WORKPLACE ASSESSMENT

EF/92/25/EN

European Foundation
for the Improvement of
Living and Working Conditions

WORKPLACE ASSESSMENT

by
Dr Steve Simmons
Jens Stampe Øland

European Foundation
for the Improvement of
Living and Working Conditions,
Loughlinstown House,
Shankill, Co. Dublin, Ireland
Tel: +353 1 282 68 88 Fax: +353 1 282 68 88
Telex: 30726 EURF EI

Cataloguing data can be found at the end of this publication

Luxembourg: Office for Official Publications of the European Communities, 1992

ISBN 92-826-4858-3

© European Foundation for the Improvement of Living and Working Conditions, 1992.

For rights of translation or reproduction, applications should be made to the Director, European Foundation for the Improvement of Living and Working Conditions, Loughlinstown House, Shankill, Co. Dublin, Ireland.

Printed in Ireland

FOREWORD

Workplace assessment is the first stage of any action being undertaken in order to improve the work environment, whether it be correcting existing situations or designing future workplaces.

Some national regulations, and, also some European directives, require companies to undertake such assessments. The 1989 EC framework directive ref. (89/391/EEC), in particular, states that risks to workers' health and safety be assessed, including when choosing equipment and laying out workplaces.

It is in this context that the Foundation decided to review the issues connected to workplace assessment. The present report is a first step in this direction. It highlights the fact that assessing risks, and work situations in general, is not only a technical issue but also a policy one, particularly at company level. Involvement of the workforce in workplace assessment is crucial. The report also highlights the fact that comprehensive and sound risk assessment needs to cover not only physical factors of the work environment such as pollution or noise, but also organisational and social factors such as repetitiveness of tasks, time pressure and compatibility between the skills of people and their task requirements.

The Foundation would like to thank the authors of the report and the advisory coordination group, which has given important suggestions throughout the project.

The authors are:

- Dr. Steve Simmons, Health And Safety Technology And Management (HASTAM) Ltd., Birmingham
- Mr. Jens Stampe Øland, Industrial Health Service of Mid Zealand (BST), Sorø, (DK)

The members of the coordination group are:

- Ms. Dagmar Diergarten, Bundesvereinigung der Deutschen Arbeitgeberverbände, Cologne
- Mr. Horst Kloppenburg, "Industrial Medicine and Hygiene" Unit, DG V/E/2, Commission of the European Communities, Luxembourg
- Mr. Jos Mossink, TNO Institute of Preventive Health Care (NIPG-TNO), Leiden
- Prof. Frank Pot, Deputy Director, TNO Institute of Preventive Health Care (NIPG-TNO), Leiden
- Ms. Agnes Saaby, Industrial Health Service of Mid Zealand (BST), Sorø, (DK)
- Mr. Marc Sapir, Director, Trade Union Technical Bureau for Health and Safety, Brussels
- Mr. Claudio Stanzani, Sindnova, CISL, Rome

The Foundation's Research Managers responsible for the project are Pascal Paoli and Henrik Litske.

Clive Purkiss
Director

Eric Verborgh
Deputy Director

Table of contents

Page

1.	Summary: Guidelines for organising and conducting workplace and environmental assessments.	1
2.	Introduction.	8
	2.1. Aims.	9
	2.2. Target audience.	9
3.	Workplace and environmental assessment.	11
	3.1. What is an assessment?	11
	3.2. Why are assessments made?	12
	3.3. Perceptions of work environment and environment problems.	13
	3.4. What methods are used?	15
4.	Two scenarios for assessment.	18
	4.1. The problem orientated model.	18
	4.2. The planning model.	21
5.	Organisation of assessment and user participation.	26
	5.1. Assessment policy.	26
	5.2. Specifying aims and objectives.	26
	5.3. Planning the assessment process.	27
	5.4. Roles and responsibilities.	28
6.	Assessment methods.	34
	6.1. Type of assessment.	34
	6.2. Strategic assessment methods.	37
	6.3. Thematic assessment methods.	41
7.	Options for describing solutions.	47
	7.1. The Function of the solution.	48
	7.2. The Technical solution.	51

			Page
8.	Practical experience - 5 case studies.		54
	8.1.	Nilpeter A/S: Authoritarian management methods should be broken down in the planning of a new factory with open lay-out, DK.	54
	8.2.	User influence on introduction of new technology at Ringsted Dun A/S, DK.	61
	8.3.	Noise assessment and noise control at Plastmo A/S, DK.	66
	8.4.	Hazardous substances assessment and control at the Kent Chemical Company Limited, UK.	71
	8.5.	Encouraging employee participation in workplace and environmental assessment at Holden Hydroman Plc., UK.	77

Appendix I: References.
Appendix II: Industrial Hygiene Assessment Manual.
Appendix III: Assessment techniques.
Appendix IV: Experience from practice.

List of figures and illustration

		Page
1.1.	Steps in assessment activities within the company.	3
1.2.	Stages in datailed assessment.	5
3.1.	The manufacturing process and its consequences.	15
4.1.	The problem orientated model.	18
4.2.	The planning model.	22
4.3.	Analysis of different demands leading to a single briefing document.	24
5.1.	Overall timetable for assessment activities.	28
5.2.	Potential participants in assessment activities.	28
5.3.	Planning activities and definition of tasks is an important issue.	31
6.1.	Assessment methods.	35
6.2.	Example of Chase II Audit Questions.	38
6.3.	Example of Chase II health and safety audit analysis.	39
6.4.	Chase II health and safety audit performance chart.	40
6.5.	Environmental audit action plan.	41
7.1.	Description of demands to the technical solution and its function, example from noise mitigation in a joiner's workshop: Planning machine.	47
7.2.	Description of technical specifications with the focus on the source, the preventive measures or the exposure conditions.	49
7.3.	Specifications on a LOCAL EXHAUST ventilation system in the suppliers contract.	50
7.4.	Ex.: Qualitative demands for a local exhaust ventilation system.	52
7.5.	Construction of mock-up: draft grinding bench at a foundry.	53
8.1.1.	The production line at Nilpeter A/S.	55
8.1.2.	The organisational structure around the planning of "Factory P4".	56
8.1.3.	Photography: The open lay-out style plan includes the cantine.	57
8.1.4.	Essential dates concerning main planning activities for "Factory P4".	58
8.1.5.	Photography: Turning machines were noise controlled and all surfaces painted white.	59

8.1.6.	Photography: Even the vacuum cleaners had to be noise controlled.	59
8.1.7.	Photography: The foremens limitation in the central part of "Factory P4".	60
8.2.1.	The production line at Ringsted Dun A/S.	61
8.2.2.	Ringsted Dun A/S organisation with regard to work environment changes.	62
8.2.3.	Steps in the assessment of technological change.	62
8.2.4.	Photography: The dust plagued stuffing work.	63
8.2.5.	Results of dust measurement.	63
8.2.6.	Sketch of a solution.	64
8.2.7.	Photography: The final workstation.	65
8.3.1.	Production line at Plastmo A/S.	66
8.3.2.	Plastmo's organisation with regard to the work environment.	67
8.3.3.	Steps in the assessment and control activities.	68
8.3.4.	Interior view from extrusion department.	68
8.3.5.	Noise dose levels.	69
8.3.6.	The contents of the noise reduction programme.	69
8.3.7.	Photography: Damped saw in the fitting department.	70
8.3.8.	Systematical check-list.	70
8.4.1.	Organisational structure with regards to health and safety at the Kent Chemical, Ltd.	72
8.4.2.	Example of productionline safety notice.	73
8.4.3.	Rawmaterial safety data sheet.	74
8.5.1.	Organisational structure with regards to health and safety at Holden Hydroman Plc.	79
8.5.2.	Example of Personal Action Plan.	80

SUMMARY

1. GUIDE-LINES FOR ORGANISING AND CONDUCTING WORKPLACE AND ENVIRONMENTAL ASSESSMENTS

There are many reasons why companies should wish to carry out assessments of workplace quality. In all businesses from chemical works to manufacturing operations, from minerals extraction to transportation and from offices to retailing, workers' health and safety can be placed at risk from exposure to a vast range of different chemical and physical hazards. Even in situations where there are no significant risks to health and safety, the quality of the work environment can influence workers' job satisfaction and performance and is an important aspect of the image that the company projects to visitors, suppliers and customers. The impact that business activity may have upon local communities and the wider environment are also of increasing concern, not least because of increasing legislation and the adverse consequences of legal action, complaints and escalating clean-up costs.

In many cases, there will be a close link between the consequences with regard to workers safety and health, and those arising from the effects upon the local environment substances and effects, such as noise or vibration, can cause problems for workers health and comfort in the workplace, as well as causing environmental pollution once they escape beyond the perimeter of the factory. It is important, therefore, that any examination of conditions in workplaces also takes account of any possible adverse consequences to the surrounding environment. For this reason, this report examines issues affecting assessments of workplace and local environmental quality.

All companies, no matter how large or small, will inevitably experience problems or circumstances that require some form of assessment such as:

- complaints from workers or local residents about noise, fumes, safety hazards, discomfort etc.
- non-compliance with laws and regulations.
- accidents or damage to health.

In these situations, the purpose of assessment is to investigate and where appropriate resolve the cause of an existing problem. However, assessment may also be important in situations where changes are taking place such as:

- planning, design and installation of new premises, plant, equipment, systems of work organisation etc.

- changes in the specification of raw materials or process conditions.
- changes in laws or regulations.
- changes in the surrounding environment, for example the siting of new residential development near to the company premises.

In such circumstances, assessments may be valuable in helping to identify potential health, safety and environmental issues and appropriate solutions that may help to minimise any adverse effects. In some situations, there may be a requirement to undertake formal assessments of the impacts that projects may have on the environment, such as those projects falling within Annex I or Annex II of European Council Directive 85/337/EEC on the assessment of the effects of certain public and private projects on the environment. In other cases, assessments of specific environmental effects may be required by planning authorities or the official bodies in support of applications, authorisations or permits. Requirements to undertake assessments of the consequences of work activity are also formalised in European Directives such as Directive 89/391/EEC on the introduction of measures to encourage improvements in the safety and health of workers at work, which states that employers shall:

"be in possession of an assessment of the risks to safety and health at work including those facing groups of workers exposed to particular risks". (Article 9, § 1).

Traditionally, most assessments tend to focus on the levels and existance of specific workplace factors such as noise, postures, psycho-social loading, or hazardous substances. However, in many instances, the ultimate effects on worker comfort, health or safety arise from a combination of several different and sometimes inter-related factors. In other words, there is a need for a multidisciplinary approach to assessment of such problems. This requires the selection of appropriate assessment methods, but more importantly it necessitates effective organisation of assessment activities, and in particular, the selection of an inter disciplinary team.

In accordance with legislation, the employers have the obligation to provide a safe and healthy place of work and ensure that their operations are conducted with minimum adverse impact on the environment. A key recommendation of this report, is that this can only be achieved where there is a clear structure within which the assessment can be conducted.

Whether external assessors are involved or not, the assessment activities can be described as characteristic stages in which the decisions are made:

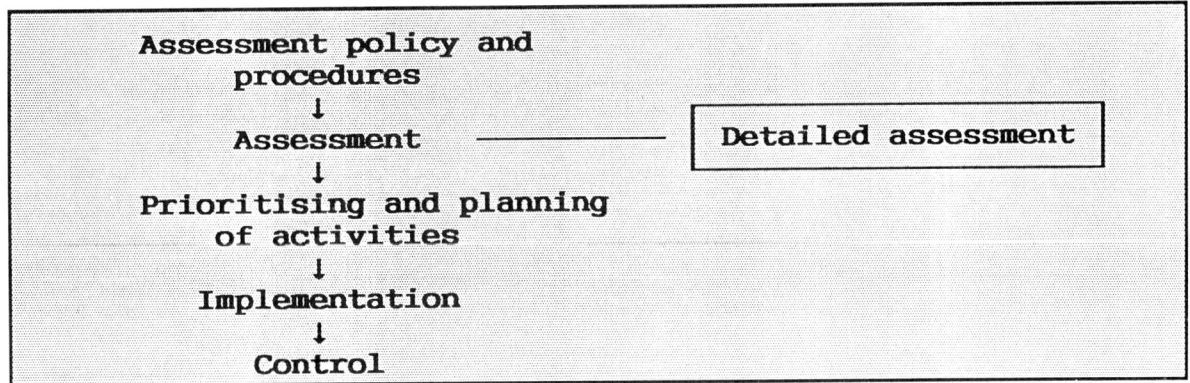

Fig. 1.1. *Steps in assessment activities within the company.*

The best approach to organising workplace or environmental effects assessments is to tackle problems step-by-step. This will involve two basic phases. The first important phase has to do with the <u>assessment policy</u> of the company and the procedures for conducting an assessment. The company will need to ensure that there is an appropriate framework which will help them to decide whether an assessment is needed and if so what the aims of the assessment should be and who will be responsible for conducting the assessment (the assessor). The next important phase should be the actual assessment itself. It is obvious that a lot of workplace and environment problems are tackled by the company itself without further investigation, i.e. by the Managers and Safety Committees, but some problems needs further investigation in the form of <u>detailed assessment</u>.

Clarification of the assessment policy and procedures is an important issue for companies to resolve. Key elements are; ensuring assessment activities are conducted systematically; involving the employees at all stages and to improve the use of assessors.

PHASE 1: ASSESSMENT POLICY AND PROCEDURES: PREPARING A BRIEF.

The aim of the first phase should be for the company to establish appropriate procedures for identifying problems, deciding whether or not action may be required and then preparing a brief for the assessor. The following issues should be taken into account:

- Who is responsible for identifying problems and what are the roles of Managers, Employees, Safety Committees, Trade Unions Advisers, Enforcing Authorities, the Public etc.
- What are the company's policies and how do these affect the problem and the assessment? Examples of policy issues that relate to the problem or the assessment of it include: human resources management; systems of work organisation; communications; training, information and education; industrial relations; financial management etc.
- How do you know that a problem exists? Problems may be identified in a variety of ways including: findings of audits, inspections or monitoring; complaints; accidents or

illness; insurance claims; consultation with staff or the public etc.
- What is the problem? Problems should be clearly defined in terms of their symptoms and their consequences and the possible underlying causes. The scale of the problem should also be estimated at this stage.
- What are the objectives? The objectives should be a straightforward description of what the parties involved are trying to achieve, such as a safe and healthy work environment, production targets, compliance with the law etc. There may be conflicting objectives between different groups, for example the worker may have different aspirations to a manager.
- Is the problem significant? Having defined the company's policies, the problem and the objectives of those concerned, initial criteria can be defined against which the extent and severity of the problem can be measured. This will enable the company to decide the relative priorities to be given to different problems. Where there are a number of problems, these should be ranked in order of significance so that efforts can be directed to areas where greatest benefit can be gained. The views of the workforce and local communities will be important criteria in deciding which problems to tackle.

If the problem is considered to be significant, it will then be necessary to think about the following:

- Who will conduct the assessment? The role of assessor may be performed by: an individual manager or employee; a designated group of workers, managers and employees; consultants or specialist advisers; or by a combination of those above.
- What skills will be required for the assessment? Assessors may need to be skilled in negotiation, consultation, organisation and technical disciplines. The key skill will be the ability to ask the right questions and to ensure that appropriate answers are obtained. The assessor may not necessarily have the skills to undertake detailed technical tasks, but should know when specialist advice is required and where this may be obtained.
- How is the assessment to be conducted? There may be many different types and levels of assessment. It is important that the right one is chosen. All assessments will provide an answer, but the company must be sure that the chosen assessment is the one which is capable of producing the best answer. Deciding what is best will entail a searching review of the policies and the aspirations of the different groups involved, as well as the constraints within which the solution will have to operate. It may also be appropriate to establish mechanisms to actively involve those who have an interest in or are affected by the problem. Active participation will help to ensure that the assessor considers all points of view and that everyone is aware of what is being done and how they may contribute. In certain circumstances, there may be a need for confidentiality

(such as medical information, personal views or opinions etc). There may be conflicts between the desire to encourage active participation in the assessment and the need to maintain privacy.
- What are the targets for the assessment? The targets may include: time schedules; resources available for conducting the assessment; resources available for the solution to the problem; performance targets; participation of workers or the public etc.

Once this information has been assembled it should be summarised in the brief that is then given to the person or group responsible for undertaking the detailed assessment. Information should also be made available to those affected by the problem and their roles in the assessment should be explained.

PHASE 2: DETAILED ASSESSMENT

The detailed assessment phase should aim to investigate the problem, its symptoms, effects and causes and then to identify possible solutions. Once potential solutions have been identified, these should be appraised so that the best solution can be chosen. The outcome of the assessment will be the recommendations. The decision about whether or not to implement the recommendations should be made by the person(s) who are responsible for the issue under investigation. Once the decision has been made, the solution can be implemented and and then monitored and evaluated to ensure that it has been effective in solving the problem. The assessor or group conducting the original assessment may also be involved in overseeing the implementation of the solution and in monitoring and evaluating its effectiveness.

```
Identify the problem
         ↓
Define detailed criteria
         ↓
  Obtain information
         ↓
Evaluate the information
         ↓
Identify options of control
         ↓
      Appraisal
         ↓
Implement the solution
         ↓
       Control
```

Fig. 1.2. Stages in detailed assessment.

The assessment should be conducted systematically and should cover the following:

<u>Identify the problem</u>. The assessor should investigate the problem in detail. The characteristics of the problem should be clearly understood. Where possible, the symptoms, effects and possible causes should be identified. There may also be links between several different problems (for example employee exposure to toxic fumes may be the result of contamination of raw materials which is in turn causing problems for process control, quality etc). Such linkages should be identified at an early stage.

Define detailed criteria against which the problem can be assessed. Criteria are important as these will enable the assessor to evaluate the significance of the problem when measured against predetermined standards. Examples of criteria would include quantitative measures such as air quality standards (TLV's, OEL's or environmental standards), biological exposure limits and noise exposure limits as well as qualitative criteria such as legal requirements, policy requirements, established working practices etc.

Obtain information. Information may be obtained by measurement, observation, inspection, reviews of data and records, interviews, modelling or prediction. In some cases there will be a need to obtain specialist advice or services, such as monitoring employee exposure to noise or fumes, health surveillance, ecological studies etc. Care should be taken to ensure that the information obtained is relevant to the problem and is sufficiently detailed to allow the relationships between the causes and the effects to be established. The views of those affected by the problem should also be considered as important information.

Evaluate the information. Having obtained the necessary factual information, the assessor should compare the data against the predetermined criteria and any other relevant considerations in order to evaluate the problem. The evaluation should aim, where possible, to highlight the relationship between the causes and the effects so that predictions can be made of the impact of any changes that may be introduced. For example, measurements of employees exposure to noise should also be linked to information about how much noise is given off by the machinery that they are working with so that the likely effects of introducing noise controls can be estimated.

Identify options for controlling the problem. The results of the evaluation will have given valuable information about the relationship between the problem and its causes. This will allow the identification of possible options for reducing or eliminating the problem.

Appraisal. The assessor should compare the likely costs, effectiveness and practical value of each option in order to identify the one which represents good value for money and best satisfies the objectives set by the company. This information should be made available to all concerned so that their views may be taken into account. The outcome of the appraisal will be a recommendation to the person responsible for the decision. This person would be expected to review the information about the assessment and the appraisal together with the views of all concerned, and then to make the decision either to implement the recommended solution or to take some other course of action.

Implement the solution. This may involve many aspects such as re-designing methods of work, training, personal protective equipment, changing processes, or introducing control measures. Some solutions may require the purchase of equipment or machinery and in these cases it is important that the designer or supplier fully understands the nature of the problem and the specifications that are required in order to resolve the problem. The assessor may be involved in the production of specifications and negotiations with designers and suppliers.

<u>Monitor and evaluate</u> the effectiveness of the solution. Monitoring of the performance of the solution is important. Regular tests or inspections should be performed to ensure that the solution meets its specifications. Evaluation means that the company undertakes and assessment of how well the solution has met the original objectives and whether new problems have arisen.

2. Introduction

The quality of peoples working environment is an important issue for all companies to consider, no matter how small they may happen to be. People are unlikely to perform effectively and efficiently if they are required to work in poor conditions. Bad lighting, poor working postures, safety hazards, extremes of temperature or exposure to hazardous substances are all examples of factors that may contribute to a low quality working environment. The ultimate cost to employers failing to ensure adequate work environments could include prosecutions, insurance claims, increased employee absence through sickness and injury. The costs to the workers may include long term disablement, disease, psychological problems or at worst death or serious injury. Similar issues apply to the effects that a company's operations may have upon the environment. The impact of emissions, discharges, wastes, spillages or leaks and other effects such as noise and vibration may adversely affect company success through prosecutions, heavy costs associated with clean-up operations, poor public image and difficulties in obtaining planning permissions, etc.

One of the main ways in which companies can identify, set priorities and resolve problems in the workplace or in the general environment is to undertake an assessment. However, this is not always as easy as it may appear. The process of organising and undertaking an assessment of a problem may raise many issues for small to medium sized companies. If insufficient thought and planning is devoted to deciding what an assessment is trying to achieve, who should be involved and how the results will be used, it is likely that the assessment will fail to resolve the problem or could even create new problems elsewhere.

With a growing body of legislation within the EC and elsewhere that requires companies to undertake assessments of health, safety or environmental aspects of their operations, it is important that all those who may be involved are aware of the potential benefits and pitfalls associated with the process of assessing problems. It for this reason that this project has been undertaken.

The main findings of the report have already been summarised in Section 1 in the form of guidance to companies and those involved in conducting and managing assessments. Section 3 sets out some basic definitions of assessment and discusses the reasons why assessments are undertaken and the general methods that may be used. In Section 4 we then go on the consider two different situations in which assessments may be of value, firstly in resolving existing problems and secondly in designing new projects to ensure that problems are not created. In Section 5, the roles of responsibilities of different groups who may be involved in assessment are examined, and particular attention is given to the organising assessment so that those affected by problems can actively participate. A review of a range of different types of assessment methodology is presented in Section 6 and issues connected to implementing solutions to problems are examined in Section 7. Finally in Section 8, we have presented five case studies to show how different companies have approached a range of assessment problems.

2.1 AIMS

The main focus of the project has been to develop a framework which can be used by companies to structure and organise workplace and environmental assessment. In particular, the project has sought to describe approaches and methods that can be used to ensure that assessments are integrated with the process of designing solutions to problems.

Specifically, the aims have been:

a) to describe the main methods that may be used by companies to identify, analyse and appraise workplace and environmental problems.
b) to identify and describe ways in which companies can make more effective use of workplace and environmental assessment within the process of planning and designing solutions to problems.

This report present the main findings of the project and suggests practical ways in which companies and those involved in assessing workplace and environmental quality can improve the value and effectiveness of such assessments. The suggestions that are made focus on ways of organising assessment activities, establishing assessment policies, using different assessment methods, communicating solutions and structuring assessment checklists/manuals. It is hoped that the recommendations and information included in this report will help companies to tackle complex, as well as simple, work and external environmental problems.

2.2 TARGET AUDIENCE

Most larger companies will have ready access to specialist expertise and sufficient internal resources and experience to overcome many day-to-day workplace and environmental problems. Experience shows that assessments pose the greatest problems for small to medium sized companies with between 10 to about 200 employees. Companies in this size range rarely have specialist in-company expertise. However, many companies of this size will undoubtedly experience problems that require some form of assessment, and this can pose significant difficulties. Therefore, to ensure that the project is of greatest value, the target audience has been defined as small to medium sized enterprises, and in particular the following groups who may participate in workplace or environmental assessments:

a) Members of Safety Committees and Safety Groups, internal technical staff and managers.
b) Advisory agencies such as employers and employees advisory organizations including Trade Unions, Industrial Health Services, Labour Inspections and enforcing authorities.

c) Consultants including specialists in buildings, technology, safety and health, and the environment.

3. Workplace and environmental assessment

In this section the basic concepts underlying the study will be explained. The purpose is to elucidate the relationship between workplace and external environments and the assessment of problems in these areas, and then to develop a simple framework for workplace and environmental assessment.

3.1 WHAT IS AN ASSESSMENT?

Assessment is a systematic process in which problems are identified, investigated and resolved.

A basic distinction must be drawn between the concepts of assessment, evaluation and appraisal.

Evaluation is normally taken to denote a particular assessment process which has the aim of establishing the effectiveness of solutions in meeting their original design objectives. Evaluation in this sense, takes place once a solution has been applied. However evaluation may also mean an assessment procedure whereby the information arising from an investigation is subject to detailed scrutiny in order to establish the significance of findings set against the initial objectives of the study and the relevant criteria that have been set. In both senses, evaluation implies a process of formally quantifying the significance of data or actions that have been taken.

Appraisal denotes a stage in the assessment procedure which encompasses the defining of objectives, examining options and weighing up their costs and benefits before deciding which solution is likely to offer the best value for money. Appraisal may therefore follow an evaluation which defines the significance of a problem, and evaluation may then follow appraisal once a solution has been implemented in order to test the effectiveness of that solution.

Assessment is taken to mean the entire process through which problems are identified, investigated and resolved and an assessment process may comprise stages in which evaluation and appraisal methodologies are used. Assessment may also be seen as an iterative process in many situations where initial assessments lead to the adoption of measures which then give rise to the need for further assessments.

There are a great many different types of assessment method. Furthermore, the situations in which assessments are performed are also highly variable. Therefore, whilst it is possible to describe these in general terms, it is difficult, if not impossible, to say which particular methods should be used in every circumstance.

3.2 WHY ARE ASSESSMENTS MADE?

The most common situation in which workplace or environmental assessment may be applied is in the investigation and evaluation of the quality of existing workplace or external environmental conditions. The objective of such assessments is to identify potential problems, investigate the nature, extent and severity of problems, to identify potential solutions and then to implement the solution representing the best value for money, which will be the solution that is most likely to be effective, efficient and economical. In many situations, the outcome of an assessment will also have to meet the criterion of being politically acceptable to the various groups involved in decision making and operation of the solution.

All companies, no matter how large or small, will inevitably experience problems or circumstances that require some form of assessment such as:

- complaints from workers or local residents about noise, fumes, safety hazards, discomfort etc.
- non-compliance with laws and regulations.
- accidents or damage to health.

In these situations, the purpose of assessment is to investigate and where appropriate resolve the cause of an existing problem.

Assessments may also be performed in circumstances where there is desire to improve workplace or environmental quality in response to organizational goals and policy frameworks.

However, assessment may also be important in situations where changes are taking place such as:

- planning, design and installation of new premises, plant, equipment, systems of work organisation etc.
- changes in the specification of raw materials or process conditions.
- changes in laws or regulations.
- changes in the surrounding environment, for example the siting of new residential development near to the company premises.

In such circumstances, assessments may be valuable in helping to identify potential health, safety and environmental issues and then to find ways to minimise or eliminate these problems by changing the existing systems, plant, equipment or procedures or the designs of proposed buildings, plant or equipment.

The way in which assessments are traditionally used by companies to resolve workplace or environmental problems, depends to a large extent on the way in which problems are perceived.

3.3 PERCEPTIONS OF WORK ENVIRONMENT AND ENVIRONMENT PROBLEMS

Traditionally, the perception of the quality of workplaces and the effects of a company's activities on the wider environment has focused on the those aspects which are directly related to adverse consequences for health and safety or environmental contamination. Therefore, much attention has been given to the effects of noise, dust, hazardous substances, illumination, thermic climate and so on. For many of these factors, elaborate criteria have been developed which form the basis of assessments designed to find out whether or not conditions are likely to give rise to adverse consequences. Examples of such criteria would include:

- occupational exposure limits such as TLV's (Treshold Limit Values), OES's (Occupational Exposure Standards).
- environmental air quality standards such as the EEC limits for lead, sulphur dioxide, smoke and nitrogen dioxide.
- noise exposure standards.

The existence of such criteria tends to focus assessment activity towards those factors which can be quantified and for which identifiable criteria have been developed. These are normally treated as single issues. Thus, individual assessments may be undertaken for many specific factors, each being performed in isolation from one another. However, as the World Health Organisation have pointed out:

"Health is a state of complete physical, mental and social well-being, and not merely the absence of disease or infirmity." (1)

This suggests that in assessing workplace or external environmental conditions, it is the overall quality of the working or living environment that is most important. For workers engaged in a particular task, their perception of workplace quality is likely to be influenced by a great number of factors, many of which may interact with one another. Poor working conditions can often be the result of the combination of factors, which if taken in isolation from one another would not be considered to be unacceptable. Only when these are added together is there a significant adverse effect on working conditions. In many cases, assessments that are undertaken fail to recognise this aspect of the nature of complex problems. This poses a significant limitation as the assessments that are conducted which focus mainly on the levels or existence of individual factors. It is essential that in tackling such problems, the multidisciplinary aspects should be taken into account. This means that often, there is a need for assessment methods which are based on information/investigations covering a range of disciplines, eg. technical, social and medical. In this report, the ergonomically based assessment is seen as one method, which is based on a multidisciplinary approach which implicitly recognises the interactions between a range of factors.

"The ergonomic can be defined as a method by which you, based on knowledge and findings from a number of scientific disciplins, investigate the problems between the human and the environment in

which it lives and works; the purpose is threw investigation and research to provide living and working conditions, which is in better harmony with the abilities and limitations of the human". (2)

While it is a weakness in many assessments that a multidisciplinary approach is not made, it is a further weakness, that the balance of the effort is directed towards investigating the levels of particular factors and measures that can be taken to alleviate any problems rather than addressing the underlying causes. For example, the outcome of an assessment of complaints by an employee about high levels of noise may be that the employee is issued with hearing protection, but without any consideration being given to the cause of the high levels of noise. Assessments are more likely to result in effective solutions if they also take into account the relationships between the effects (that is to say the factors and their likely consequences) and the causes (the manufacturing process).

To emphasise the need for a multidisciplinary approach which aims to take action on the cause of the problem, we shall in the following describe an overall framework for concepts, methods and approaches to assessment of work environment and environment.

The manufacturing process can be divided into four characteristic elements: (3)

1. The technical system which denotes the buildings, machinery, tools, chemical additives, etc.
2. The people.
3. Raw materials.
4. The systems of work organisation and management, i.e. roles and responsibilities, division of labour, company policies and procedures, systems of work, etc.

The manufacturing process is closely linked to working and environmental conditions. This is represented in Fig. 3.1. (p.15) which illustrates the relationship between the manufacturing process, the work environment or environmental factors and their ultimate consequences.

Describing assessment methods, the connection between the manufacturing process, the working and environment conditions (factors) and the impact on health and safety and environment is important. The manufacturing process is designed and influenced by the decision makers. At company level important decision makers are: The owner, the technicians, the local manager, the operators and their representatives. External decisions may also influence the design of the manufacturing process, such as those made by suppliers of machinery and raw materials as well as external consultants.

This forms a useful framework within which the concept and approaches to assessment can be developed and will be expanded throughout this report.

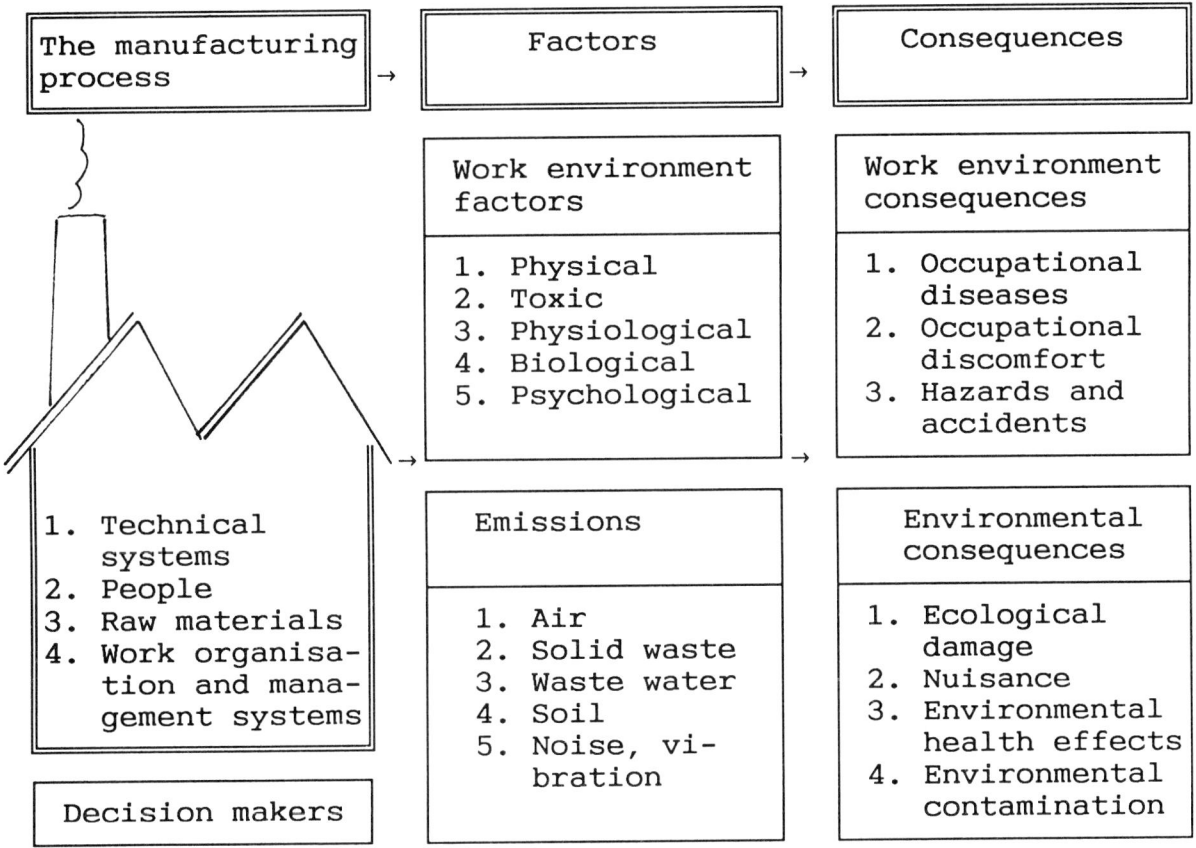

Fig. 3.1. The manufacturing process and its consequences.

In this connection it is very common to view work environment factors and consequences in only quantitative terms, ie. they are measureable. Therefore it must be stressed that it is our perception that the basic concepts can also be assessed from a qualitative viewpoint based on knowledge of the causes of the problems. This is particularly important where assessment concerns work environment problems related to work organisation and poor psycho-social working conditions. In such cases a wide range of qualitative aspects of the workplace must be assessed, i.e., stress related to overdemanding work, the monotonous work environment related to work with no challenges to the employee and the degree of social contact and cooperation as factors which can reduce the loads.

3.4 WHAT METHODS ARE USED?

In deciding what type of assessment should be conducted there are several important issues which should be considered. Firstly there is the policy framework which operates within the company. Assessments often have a bearing on or are influenced by policies such as industrial relations, finance, employment, etc. Companies may also have specific policies which govern how and in what circumstances assessments are conducted. Not all assessment methods will be neutral within these policy frameworks and selection of methods should take account of this factor. Secondly, consideration should be given to the people involved in or who may be affected by the assessment. Workers or local residents may be directly affected by the problem and by any solutions that may be identified. Their views will be an important dimension which should be integral to the assessment process. Thirdly, the assessment method will clearly have to be appropriate to the nature of the problem under investigation. A balance must be achieved between the competing pressures to obtain as much information as possible and the practical constraints of time and resources. Fourthly, it depends on the aim of the assessment. These issues have to do with the involvement of decision makers in assessment activities, or in other words: the organisation of assessment at company level, which will be explored in more detail in Section 5.

The division of work environment problems in terms of the cause of the problem in the manufacturing process, the factors and their consequences as discussed in the preceding sub-section is useful when it comes to describing particular methods that can be employed as tools to aid workplace and environmental assessment. There are a wide variety of different types of methods that can be used in investigating workplace or environmental problems. Some focus on information relevant to the causal elements of problems (ie the source of the problem), some on workplace or environmental factors and others on the consequences for health, safety and the environment. These will be explored in more detail in Section 6.

Some types of assessment may entail using just one main method of data gathering and analysis. In many situations however, the characteristics of the problem may require several different approaches in order to obtain sufficient information to allow an appropriate assessment. For example, complaints about noise at work stations may involve the following methods in the assessment:

The manufacturing process;
- Analysis of technical information on the machinery etc
- Analysis of systems of work
- Investigation of the building structure.

Work environment factors;
- measurement of noise emission levels and frequencies
- measurement of employee noise doses
- examination of production and work records

Work environment consequences;
- analysis of audiograms to detect hearing damage.
- interviewing workers to identify consequences etc.

Potential solutions may involve changes to the source of the noise emission, altering work schedules or providing hearing protection. In general, the more robust solutions are those that aim to eliminate or reduce the problem at source. This applies to equally to both workplace and external environmental problems.

When the outcome of an assessment is to initiate preventive action, the subsequent work to design a solution can be done by experts, by the company itself or as a result of dialog. The processes which facilitate the design of solutions and the communication of information between assessors, the company and designers/suppliers are explored in more detail in Section 7.

4. Two scenarios for assessment

In the preceding section, the two different scenarios within which assessments may be conducted have been introduced. These are the assessment of existing environmental or workplace conditions and assessments conducted during situations where changes are taking place such as the planning or designing of new buildings, plant, systems of work etc.

In the first scenario, the assessment takes as its focus the identification and resolution of problems that already exist. In such circumstances, the assessment may be seen to be a relatively discrete process which can be represented in terms of a simple model referred to as the problem orientated model.

In the second scenario, assessments may be conducted with the aim of forecasting the likely consequences for workplace or environmental quality that can be expected within a given situation where changes are taking place. The reasons for change are often technical or financial. In such situations, assessments are integrated within the overall planning/design process which shall be represented in this section by a simple planning model.

4.1 THE PROBLEM ORIENTATED MODEL

From the discussion in the preceding sections, it is clear that workplace and environmental assessments per se may comprise many different stages, each of which serves a different purpose. Examination of the wide variety of different "assessments" that are commonly applied in workplace situations reveals that irrespective of the type of assessment and the problem being investigated, there are several identifiable and common stages through which all assessments must progress if a satisfactory solution is to emerge. These distinct stages can be represented by a simple model which can be simply referred to as "the problem orientated model".

The problem orientated model consists of six component stages as shown in Figure 4.1

```
            STAGE    ACTIVITY

     ┌─ 1'   1        Problem identification
     │       2        Problem analysis
  Feedback   3        Identification and appraisal of options
     │       4        Decision
     │       5        Implementation
     └─────  6        Operation of the solution
```

Figure 4.1. The problem orientated model

Stage 1: Problem Identification

The first stage - problem identification - requires that the problem issue is recognised and accepted at all levels within the company and necessary factual data are assembled in order that the characteristics of the problem can be determined. In some cases the problem may be relatively simple, for example high levels of noise which are causing adverse consequences for health or comfort. In other cases problems may be complex and result from a combination of many factors, such as poor work performance arising from: poor design, workplace hazards, environmental conditions, etc. Whatever the problem, it is essential that sufficient information is obtained in order that the problem itself can be recognised and adequately described so that potential causal factors can be identified. This stage of an assessment may also extend to situations where problems are not immediately apparent and can only be recognised through the systematic recording and investigation of information on sickness, safety performance, environmental conditions, accident records, insurance claims, complaints from workers or the public etc. To detect potential problems before their consequences become apparent, companies may make use of prospective assessment methods of investigation and analysis. For example, adverse consequences for health or the environment arising from the use of substances may be revealed by monitoring of health or environmental conditions and gathering information from other sources such as journals, official publications etc. A significant change in the TLV or OES of a substance may trigger a reassessment of the risks arising from use of the substance in the workplace. In this case a problem may be identified following an initial screening or a brief assessment which can then trigger a full formalised assessment corresponding to the problem orientated model. The role of prospective assessment methods is discussed in more detail in Section 6.

Stage 2: Problem analysis

The second stage in the model is the analysis of the causes of the problem which may include <u>gathering detailed information</u> on the problem and its causes, <u>defining criteria</u> and on basis of this an <u>evaluation</u> of the severity of the problem can be made in order to assess the nature, extent and magnitude of the problem and its underlying causes. At this stage sufficient information should be obtained in order that relationships between the various causal factors can be established. For example, if the problem is one of excess noise, the information required may include:

- observations of noise, its impact and behavioural factors which may affect noise emission or worker exposure;
- discussions with workers about their perceptions of the problem;
- measurements of workplace noise levels, source emission levels and frequency analysis;
- analysis of equipment designs, condition and effectiveness of any controls;

In some cases, the nature of the change may be the introduction of standard technology, for example the purchase of new tools or equipment. In these circumstances, the planning/design process focuses upon the defining of user requirements and demands, appraisal of purchase options, arranging contracts with suppliers and then overseeing installation and commissioning.

In other situations, the change may be more complex and may go through many cycles as the project progresses. For example, in the planning and design of a new building, the project progresses from an initial outline concept through ever more detailed proposals until the final designs are completed.

This raises in interesting problem, namely how can assessments linked to health, safety and the environment be integrated within a highly variable and dynamic planning and design process. Again it is helpful if the planning and design process is represented by a simple step-by-step model which has five key stages as shown in Figure 4.2. (4)(5)(6)

STAGE	ACTIVITY
1 BRIEFING	- Consultation with interested groups. - Analysis of users needs and demands. - Establishing priorities. - Initial costings, schedules and timetables.
2 PROPOSALS	- Establishing main options. - Appraisal of options. - Recommendations. - Decisions.
3 FINALISATION	- Detailed projections and schedules. - Preparation of final plans. - Liaison with authorities. - Estimation of quantities, etc. - Contract and tender documents. - Costings and award of contracts.
4 IMPLEMENTATION	- Construction/delivery. - Installation. - Commissioning. - Instruction/training.
5 APPLICATION	- Evaluation against initial specification. - Operation/use. - Maintenance. - Re-assessment where necessary.

While this model is presented as a sequential process, in complex projects consisting of many specific phases, there will be reiteration and feedback loops between the various stages.

It is important that health, safety and environmental issues are considered early on in the briefing stage of the planning and design process and at all subsequent stages. Early involvement will help to ensure that relevant issues are identified and taken into account in any decisions that are taken and before options are ruled out. It is progressively more difficult to influence a project the further through the planning process that issues are raised.

At the start point of the planning process it is important to clarify aims and objectives overall timetables, tasks, roles and responsibilities of the many parties involved. This is described in detail in Section 5.

The role of health, safety and environmental assessment within the planning model can be summarised as follows.

Stage 1: Briefing

The main focus of the briefing stage is to identify the demands and constraints that surround the proposed change. Demands may include: the production requirements in terms of performance, size, quantity, quality etc; user requirements such as ease of use and safety; legislative demands; qualitative demands such as colour, design style etc. Constraints may include; cost; time; resources; space; integration with existing processes and operations; avoidance of adverse environmental impact etc.

The outcome of the briefing stage will be description of the performance criteria against which various options can be tested. The health, safety and environmental demands and constraints must be taken into account at this stage if the best option is to be selected. Examples of health, safety and environmental demands and constraints would include:

- legislative exposure limits such as TLV's, OES's, or environmental standards.
- standards and guide-lines on construction, guarding, electrical safety, labelling and warning signs, emergency access and egress etc.
- environmental constraints such as avoidance of damage to protected habitats or species, groundwater protection, avoidance of nuisance, minimum transport impact etc.
- planning conditions or regulations.
- working conditions such as accessibility, temperature, lighting, odour, dust etc.
- waste and effluent generation and disposal requirements and costs.
- atmospheric emission limits and control costs.
- noise and vibration emission and transmission levels.
- hazards such as flammability, explosion, etc.
- low risk of exposure to hazardous substances or effects including chemical, physical or biological hazards.
- ease of maintenance and operation.
- emergency operation and control.

This is the single most important stage and it is important that health, safety and environmental issues are identified. Participation in this process by all groups of users is clearly one way of helping to improve the eventual outcome.

In many cases there will be areas of conflict or incompatibility between the needs or demands of different groups. For example, workers may view a project in terms of ease of use and safety while managers may be primarily concerned with output, quality, etc. In order to ensure that these demands and constraints may be defined it is important to encourage active participation of all groups likely to be affected by the change. The different demands and constraints must be brought together so that priorities can be decided and a single briefing document prepared, i.e. as illustrated in Figure 4.3. (4)(7)

Fig. 4.3. *Analysis of different demands leading to a single briefing document.*

The outcome of this stage will be used as the basis of the appraisal of options so it is important that the brief is easily understandable and expresses the demands and constraints in an unambiguous way. The initial brief will also be an important document against which the success or failure of the project will eventually be evaluated. It is often helpful if these demands and constraints are summarised in the form of a simple check-list which can then be used to test possible design options.

Stage 2: Proposals

The second element of the planning and design process is the identification of potential design options. Initially there may be several principal options which once decided, will then govern all subsidiary options. For example, a power station may be powered by gas, coal, oil or nuclear fuel. The decision as to the type of energy source will radically affect all other aspects of the project. Using the check-list of demands and constraints, it may be possible at this stage to review each principal option and identify those that are most likely to meet the requirements of the brief. This may entail performing individual assessments of the projected effects associated with each option. However, the methods that are used to gather information as the basis of the assessment will be largely predictive and may include modelling, predictions, scale models, observing similar projects elsewhere, judgements based on experience etc. The outcomes of these initial assessments can then be appraised in order to identify the best options as the basis of recommendations and then decisions.

Once the most favourable option(s) have been identified, there will then be series of subsidiary options which can each be assessed in turn with the outcomes being compared against the initial brief. In this way the project design options are progressively refined.

Again it will be beneficial to encourage user participation throughout the process of refining the design proposals. Consultation with potential suppliers, regulatory bodies, the local community and all other groups affected by or with an interest in the project may also be important.

For some types of development project, there may requirements to undertake formal environmental assessments as set out in the EC Directive 85/337/EEC on the assessment of the effects of certain public and private projects on the environment.

Stage 3: Finalisation

During this stage the technical details of the chosen design solution are finalised as technical calculations, descriptions and drafts. On the basis of this information the authorities can evaluate the project. Detailed costings are prepared at this stage.

The requirements are set out in draft contracts and tender documents[1]. The ability of tenderers to provide goods and services with minimum risks to health, safety and the environment may also be taken into account in the process of selecting contractors/suppliers.

Stage 4: Implementation

Once this stage has been reached, the possibilities for influencing a project are limited. However, monitoring of the project to ensure health, safety and environmental protection may be important.

Stage 5: Application

Once the project is completed and operational, the outcome can be evaluated against the original check-list of demands and constraints as well as other criteria such as finance, performance etc. The lessons learnt may help to improve future projects and assessment.

---

[1] In some cases the tender make take place at an earlier stage, i.e. when dealing with construction companies covering advisorly activities in the planning process as well as the construction activities.

5. Organisation of assessment and user participation

In the preceding Section 4, two different scenarios in which assessments may be undertaken have been described in terms of the stages through which problems are identified and then resolved. By viewing assessment as a systematic process in this way, it is evident that companies should have in place clearly defined and unambiguous procedures designed to ensure that assessments are organised effectively. In this section, the organisational aspects of health, safety and environmental assessments are examined. (4)(8)

5.1 ASSESSMENT POLICY

All companies operate within a framework of formal and informal policies. These help to guide the development of specific plans and procedures and underlie many decisions that are made at all levels within a company.

It is important that the relationship between a company's policies and an assessment of a problem are clearly understood as these may influence the way in which the assessment is conducted and may influence the eventual outcome. For example, many companies will have formalised health and safety policies which set out the objectives, procedures and responsibilities for ensuring health and safety at work. Such policies may well have an important bearing upon the assessment process, particularly in respect of: the types of problem that assessed; the roles and responsibilities of managers, employees and employee representatives; resources available for assessments and solutions to problems; and channels of communication. Companies may also have specific environmental policies which also help to guide assessment activity. Assessments may also be influenced directly or indirectly by other aspects of company policy such as finance, personnel, public relations, marketing, etc.

A further aspect of the policy environment is that policies may help to determine what priorities are attached to different problems and whether or not they are brought forward for detailed assessment.

5.2 SPECIFYING AIMS AND OBJECTIVES

Before any assessment can be initiated, the aims and objectives of the assessment should be defined. In part these will reflect the policy framework, however the views of managers, employees, employee representatives, the local community and enforcing authorities may also have an important bearing upon the aims and objectives. In many cases there will be a divergence of views. Companies should ensure that they are at least aware of the different aspirations held by parties involved in or who may be affected by a problem before commencing a detailed assessment. This will entail some form of consultation process. Clearly the nature and form of consultation will vary according to the type of problem being investigated.

Where a problem already exists, consultation may involve gathering views from those directly affected such as employees or local residents, and those who may be indirectly involved such as regulatory agencies, local authorities and special interest groups (such as environmental groups or bodies). In situations where the assessment is linked to some form of development (such as new premises or processes, design of new products or equipment, introduction of new systems of work organisation etc) or is brought about by imminent or proposed changes (such as new laws or regulations, altered specification of materials or process conditions or changes in the surrounding environment) consultation may be more complex as this will entail making available information on the likely effects of the changes. Such circumstances may also require consultation with other bodies such as customers, suppliers, etc.

The process of consulting with other parties will also help to clarify the nature of problems or potential problems. Other people may have different perspectives that may help to point to potential causes, effects or consequences that have so far gone unrecognised.

Having established the views of the different groups, aims and objectives can then be determined. Where there are conflicting views, an attempt should be made to reconcile these so that the assessment stands the greatest chance of producing an outcome that is acceptable to those affected whilst still providing a solution that is compatible with the needs of the company and its policies, plans and strategies.

A further aspect of the aims of assessment is that very often there will be a number of potential problems which could be brought forward for detailed assessment. It is important in such situations that assessment effort is directed to those problems which merit attention and will give the greatest return in terms of benefits. Some mechanism needs to be in place which allows a company to prioritise problems and the order that they are tackled.

5.3 PLANNING THE ASSESSMENT PROCESS

In cases where an assessment is relatively simple and straightforward, the order in which tasks are undertaken and the timing of the assessment may be relatively clear. In more complex situations, or where an assessment is part of a wider project (such as designing new premises or processes), it is essential that there is a clear plan which provides a framework for the assessment process. Issues that may need to be considered include:

- Definition of tasks and how long these are expected to take.
- The requirements for any solution such as whether this will be constructed or developed in-company or by contract with

suppliers.
- What is the overall time table for the assessment and the inputs from different groups, experts, advisers etc.

There are many techniques that can be used but one of the most simple and widely used is the Gantt-matrix such as the example shown below:

	May	June	July	Aug.
Investigation, report	▨			
Description of solutions	▨	▨		
Contracting, commissioning			▨	
Evaluation				▨
Meeting, decisions		▨	▨	▨

Fig. 5.1. Overall timetable for assessment activities.

5.4 ROLES AND RESPONSIBILITIES

Many different groups may have a role in assessments including:

WITHIN COMPANY	a.	owners
	b.	managers
	c.	technicians
	d.	employee representatives
	e.	employees
	f.	health and safety advisers
	g.	environmental advisers
ADVISORY BODIES	a.	consultants
	b.	suppliers
	c.	manufacturers
	d.	designers
	e.	trade unions
	f.	employers organisations
	g.	trade organisations
	h.	insurance companies
	i.	industrial health services
AUTHORITIES	a.	Labour
	b.	Health and Safety
	c.	Environmental Protection
	d.	Planning
	e.	Health
	f.	Environmental Health
	g.	Fire

Fig. 5.2. Potential participants in assessment activities.

In defining the roles and responsibilities of the many parties that can have an input into the assessment process, it is helpful to draw a clear distinction between the activities that are undertaken within the company and those which comprise the formal assessment process itself (as summarised in Section 4).

Coordinating and managing assessments at the company level

At the company level, a framework for managing assessments needs to be established. This may involve managers, employees, employee representatives and advisory bodies. In many companies, safety committees or groups will already be established and these can play an important part in helping to set-up and manage assessment activities. Environmental problems will tend to be handled directly by company managers and advisers, although there is an increasing trend to involve employees and their representatives in environmental activities. Some larger or more hazardous works may have established local environmental liaison groups or committees which include local authority officers, special interest groups and local residents. Depending on their status, bodies represented, expertise, and time available, such committees or groups may be appropriate bodies to coordinate and manage assessments. In other situations, it may be more appropriate to establish project groups with a specific remit to oversee assessments linked to new developments etc. Project management teams may be given the responsibility for organising and managing assessments in such circumstances.

Where companies do not have the time or necessary expertise to plan and manage assessments, external assistance may be required. Such assistance may be provided by consultants, advisory bodies, suppliers etc. Where there are conflicting views on problems or difficulties in making decisions which political implications within the company, facilitators may be brought in to help to oversee the management of the assessment process. Whatever the arrangements for managing assessments at the company level, the following roles or functions should be undertaken by one or more people:

> **Problem identification.**
> **Prioritising problems.**
> **Initial investigation of problems.**
> **Initiating assessments.**
> **Planning and managing assessments.**
> **Consulting groups involved.**
> **Resolving conflicts.**
> **Setting aims and objectives.**
> **Identifying options for assessment methods.**
> **Appointing assessors.**
> **Appointing technical advisers, consultants, experts etc.**
> **Coordination of activities.**
> **Decision making or decision referral.**
> **Overseeing implementation of solutions.**
> **Monitoring implementation of solutions.**
> **Evaluating the effectiveness of the solution.**

From experience, many of the problems that are encountered stem from poor planning and coordination of the assessment at the company level, ie this is evident in common problems such as:

- the problem solving process terminates when the company has received the report.
- decisions are not made.
- inappropriate assessment methods are used.
- important constraints such as available finance are not taken into account.
- the end users experience or views are not taken into account.
- the implemented solution is not evaluated and maintained.
- experts are given poor or inappropriate briefs.

By ensuring that the project team or group responsible for coordinating assessments have sufficient experience and resources and are able to have access to the necessary information and expertise, many of these problems can be avoided. It is also important to ensure that the role of such a group is defined, particularly in terms of their responsibility for making decisions.

The importance of consultation with groups likely to be affected by a problem and its solution has already been stressed. In many circumstances, active participation of such groups in the assessment process may help to improve the ultimate value of assessments. People are more likely to accept the outcome of an assessment and appreciate the constraints and limitations if they are actively encouraged to participate in all stages of planning and managing such an assessment. Furthermore, the end result may be more appropriate and more effective because:

- the users may provide information concerning the nature of the problem, the consequences and the relationship with potential causes.
- their views on the practicability and likely effectiveness of possible solutions can be integrated in the assessment.
- in many cases they will be required to participate in the implementation and operation of the solution.

The task of each participant and the moment at which they will be involved must be carefully planned and their responsibilities must be described. The following example is an illustration of this need:

They got a workplace assessment → but wanted a solution.

In an old mechanical workshop 4 smiths are repairing lorrys, trucks and tractors. Some days welding are the only task and on these days the air is not realy good, because of a bad functioning exhaust system. The manager call for the Industrial Health Service, which are looking for the problem by interviewing and describing the workplace and workstation. The report decumented the need for a sufficient local exhaust system and proposed fundamental solutions.
The workshop found the report useless - because they wanted a solution. The Industrial Health Service then drafted a local exhaust system which could be constructed by the smiths themselves, and within about a month the solution was applicated.

Fig. 5.3. Planning activities and definition of tasks is an important issue.

Performing assessments: the role of assessors and experts

Once a company has established an appropriate organisational structure within which assessments can be planned and managed, it is then the task of the appointed assessor(s) to undertake the detailed technical assessment of the problem and to identify possible solutions. Before the assessor can begin work it is important that they are given a specific brief which sets out the nature of the problem, any demands or constraints and the resources available for the assessment and the implementation of the solution.

The role of assessor can be performed by an individual manager or employee; a designated group of workers, managers and employees; consultants or specialist advisers; or by a combination of the above. The key skill that assessors will require is the ability to ask the right questions and to ensure that the appropriate answers are obtained. Assessors may not necessarily have the knowledge or experience to undertake all of the technical assessment tasks, but should have sufficient understanding to know when specialist advice is required and where this can be obtained from.

During the assessment of the actual problem issue, there may be a requirement for detailed specialist assistance. This role is often performed by in-house advisers or by external consultants. Their role will be to undertake detailed investigations of causes, effects or consequences. Their input may be required at all stages of the actual assessment from problem identification through to identifying options for control and implementing the chosen solution. As an example, an investigation of high levels of noise in the workplace may require some or all of the following:

- surveys of noise levels in the workplace and at work stations.
- investigation of behavioural factors such as working methods, patterns of movement etc.
- measurements of employee personal noise exposure.
- measurements of noise emission and transmission from different sources.
- assessing the impact and effectiveness of existing noise control measures.
- deciding on appropriate criteria such as noise dose levels, environmental limits, qualitative measures etc;
- assessment of noise induced hearing loss in employees.
- reviews of medical and insurance records to identify problems associated with noise on health.
- interviews with employees to assess impact of noise exposure on health, comfort and moral.
- analysis of noise measurements to identify where controls can or should be applied.
- modelling or prediction of noise attenuation likely to be achieved by different options of control.
- analysis of noise data and performance data for hearing protection equipment to select appropriate models.
- designing new methods of work to reduce noise exposure.
- designing new tools and equipment to reduce noise emission.
- testing control options.
- evaluating all of the above information to identify potential options.
- projecting costs for control options.
- producing specifications and design criteria for chosen solutions.
- liaison with suppliers.
- monitoring and evaluation of solutions as they are implemented.

It is clear that not all of these roles can be performed by a single expert and therefore several types of specialist advice would be required. This will require detailed planning and coordination to help to ensure that the correct information is given to the appointed experts, that they are consulted at the right time and that their results are brought together to give a satisfactory assessment. It will also be necessary to ensure that there are effective channels of communication so that dialogue can be established between the different experts and between the experts and the assessor and those who be responsible for any decisions.

6. Assessment methods

In Section 3, the basic concepts underlying workplace and environmental assessment have been introduced. A distinction was made between methods that aim at the investigation of causal elements of problems, the workplace and environmental factors that these give rise to and their ultimate consequences for health, safety and the environment. In this Section, the actual methods that may be used to investigate workplace or environmental problems are examined in more detail.

6.1 TYPE OF ASSESSMENT

Workplace and environmental assessments can be broadly divided into two categories depending on the purpose of the assessment and the level at which it is conducted. The first category includes those assessments which address strategic aspects of the management of health and safety or environmental risks. The second category includes a wide variety of assessment methods which are designed to examine particular aspects of health and safety or environmental matters which, for the purposes of this report, can be referred to as thematic assessments.

Strategic assessments subject all areas of a company's activities to a systematic and critical examination with the aim of reducing risks and maximising performance in health and safety and environmental management. In short, the purposes of such assessments are to allow companies to make strategic decisions and to formulate strategies. At the highest level, corporate strategy embraces those aspects of decision making which are concerned with the scope of an organisation's activities. At the corporate level, health and safety and environmental issues may be only one of many different aspects which are taken into account in the development of company strategy, they are nonetheless important factors which need to be addressed. Linked to an organisation's corporate strategy will be whole series of subsidiary operational strategies concerning for example policies, marketing, finance, manufacturing and so on. Health, safety and environmental issues may be explicitly addressed in the development of operational strategies, and may also be the subject of specific strategies as well. If an operation is producing unacceptable and avoidable impacts on health, safety or the environment, the long-term feasibility of the operation is clearly in doubt. Therefore, in the process of formulating corporate and operational strategies, managers need information about the broader scale of risks, the organisation's performance in reducing these risks and areas where improvements are required. For this reason assessments designed to identify and measure performance and risk are essential if the strategies are to be appropriate and effective.

One of the main assessment tools that have been developed to provide information in the formulation and revision of strategies is auditing. In the same way that performance in financial management can be audited regularly by a company's accountants, health and safety performance may also be subject to auditing. Health and safety audits have now been used for many years in companies throughout the EC. Environmental audits are also becoming more widely used. Initiated by high risk industries in the United States, many companies are now developing auditing systems to address environmental risks and also to identify opportunities for cost savings, new "green" products and processes, and public relations initiatives. (9)(10)(11)

In addition to strategic assessments, there are a wide variety of thematic assessments designed to identify and evaluate health, safety and environmental problems associated with particular aspects of an operation. Thematic assessments may be highly specific such as an assessment of the hazards arising from machinery or substances, the adverse effects associated with exposure to particular workplace factors such as atmospheric contamination or noise, or the impact of activities on health or the environment. Other types of thematic assessments may be broader in nature covering the interactions between several different aspects of activities such as assessments of risk or ergonomic assessments.

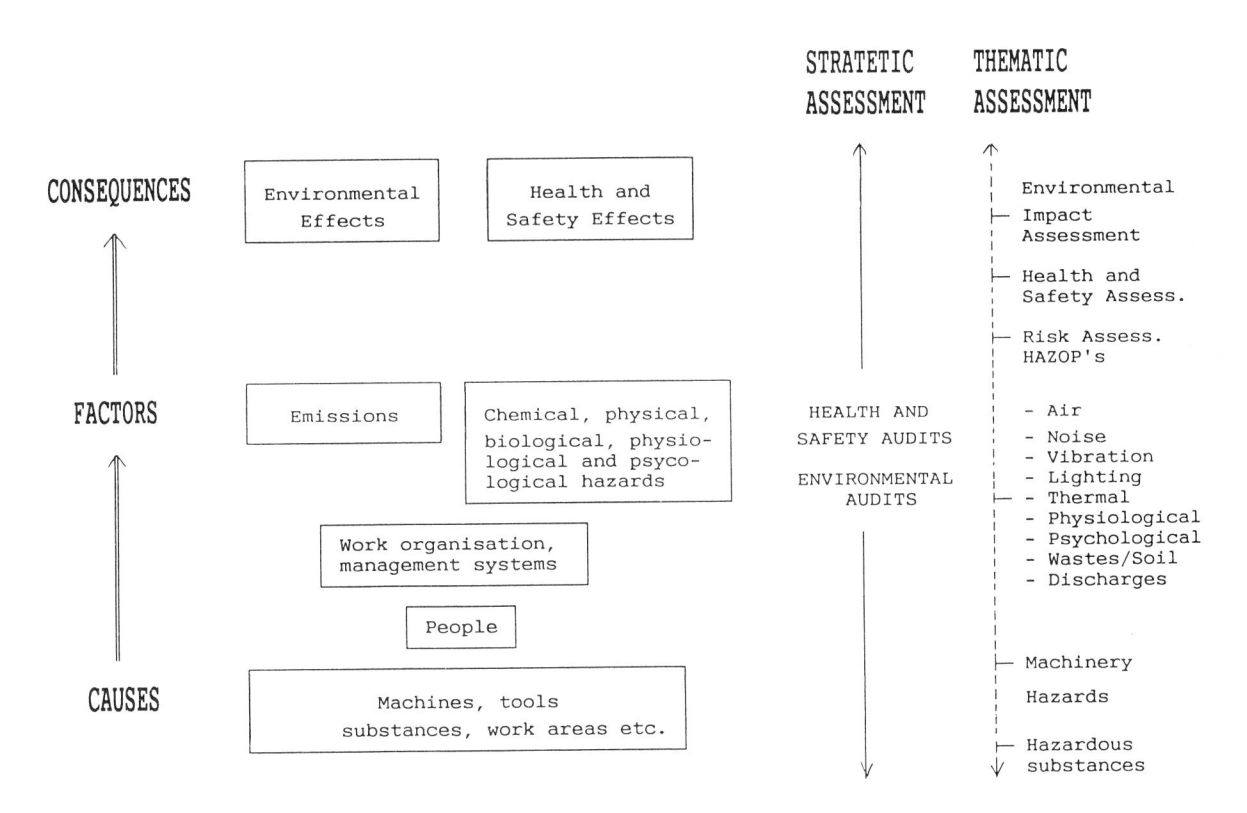

Fig. 6.1. Assessment methods.

The differences between strategic and thematic assessments are represented in Figure 6.1. Strategic assessments aim to examine the entirety of the manufacturing process from the facilities and raw materials to the eventual consequences on the environment or health and safety. Thematic assessments focus upon specific stages or a combination of stages in the manufacturing process, workplace factors and their consequences. In this report ergonomics is seen as a specific concept which views the interaction of workers and their environment as a multidisciplinary problem which may incorporate any aspect of the problem cause-factor-consequence relationship.

Strategic Assessments

The effectiveness of management of health and safety is most often assessed in terms of the avoidance of negative consequences of activities such as the absence of accidents, ill-health and so on. However, managers need to be sure that this derives from good management and not simply luck. Therefore, health and safety auditing has been developed as a proactive assessment system to provide information on the effectiveness of the company's policies, systems and procedures and also on the prevailing attitude and culture towards health and safety at all levels and at all stages of operations. Audits may examine the complete health and safety management system across all areas of activity, or may be focussed towards particular areas of responsibility or aspects of processes. The aim of an audit is to obtain an assessment of performance that embraces many aspects of health and safety management.

Health and safety audits may address compliance with policies and management systems; compliance with legislation, licensing, notification and permits; tools, equipment, fixtures and fittings; machinery and plant; use of chemicals and substances; vehicles; energy; occupational health management; training and communications; emergencies and accidents; buildings and premises; security etc.

The outputs of a health and safety audit are in the form of a detailed report that may cover:

- assessment of accidents or ill health record:
- standards of compliance with legal requirements:
- standards of compliance with the company's own health and safety policy and organisational arrangements:
- evaluation of the achievement of specific safety objectives:
- an action plan.

Audits may be repeated at regular intervals to allow an organisation to monitor progress over time and identify improvements or deterioration. Typically audits are conducted by a small team of specialists or managers from other sites and may last from a day to several days depending on there scope and level of detail. The output of the audit is typically a report detailing the findings and areas where improvements are required.

An environmental audit provides a systematic examination of the impact on the environment of all of a company's activities. It has been described as "a management tool comprising a systematic, documented, periodic and objective evaluation of how well environmental organisation, management and equipment are performing with the aim of helping to safeguard the environment by:

- Facilitating management control of environmental protection.
- Assessing compliance with company policies which would include meeting regulatory requirements". (12)

Audits may cover compliance with policies, management systems and controls; site history; regulatory compliance; licensing; permits; storage facilities; use of resources; production processes; premises; energy usage; emission to air, water and land; waste management; accident prevention and emergency procedures.

Audit reports cover broadly the same areas as a health and safety audit but with their focus on environmental management.

6.2 STRATEGIC ASSESSMENT METHODS

Health and Safety Audits

Health and safety audits usually comprise three main stages, Firstly, a plan for the audit is prepared covering the selection of the site and activities to be audited, selection of audit team members and a detailed work plan specifying the timescales, priorities and resources to be devoted to the audit. Secondly, the audit is conducted in several steps starting with the review of the management control systems, then an assessment of the effectiveness of the management control system which is supported by gathering detailed data to test and verify information given, Finally, the audit report is prepared and action plans formulated.

Many companies use in-house company check-lists to structure the audit. However, there are an increasing number of proprietary audit systems including DuPont Safety Systems, International Safety Rating System (ISRS), CHASE, British Safety Council Five Star Scheme, and COURSAFE (13). The methods used are generally based on check-lists of questions requiring simple yes/no answers or judgements about how well managers are responding to each issue. ISRS includes a check-list of around 580 detailed questions in twenty sections. Auditors validate the answers and award scores against each question based on their judgement as to the degree of compliance. The scoring system allows for different levels of attainment. Performance is evaluated by analysis of scores and overall ratings are awarded. CHASE (Complete Health And Safety Evaluation) is available either as manual or as a computerised audit system. CHASE comes in various formats, each designed to audit a particular aspect of health and safety management. CHASE II is a detailed health and safety audit covering some 400 questions each of which is given a yes/no/not applicable answer. Each question is weighted so that scores reflect the different priorities to be attached to each issue. The audit output is in the form of an action list of recommendations in priority order, and a detailed breakdown of scores for sections, parts and questions.

Figure 6.2. shows a typical set of questions from a CHASE II audit.

SECTION 4
MANAGEMENT OF CHEMICALS AND SUBSTANCES

4.4   Organisational Aspects

Answer YES or NO

4.4.a   Has a formal assessment been made of the hazards and risks posed by all the substances you listed at the beginning of this section?

4.4.b   Is there a permanent record of the assessment(s)?

4.4.c   In each case, is there a procedure to ensure that exposure to hazardous substances is either prevented or adequately controlled?

Are clearly defined systems of work with substances:

4.4.d   Laid down?

4.4.e   Followed?

4.4.f   Are there designated and clearly marked storage areas for substances?

Are there adequate procedures for:

4.4.g   Informing employees of hazardous substances?

4.4.h   Informing employees of the means by which hazards are recognised and controlled?

4.4.i   Training employees in safe systems of work with substances?

SCORE Count 5 points for each **YES** answer. Write points total below and carry it over to the next page.

TOTAL   **CARRY SCORE**

Fig. 6.2. **Example of CHASE II Audit Questions**

By answering each question, scores are allocated which are then summarised to give managers and employees a quantified assessment of how well health and safety is being managed and where the main areas of risk are. Results may be summarised in tabular form to enable problem areas to be identified (ie those areas with low scores).

SUMMARY TABLE

SUMMARY: BIRMINGHAM FEBRUARY AND JULY 1991
DATE   : 24 OCTOBER 1991   NORMAL COMPLIANCE
AUDITOR: HASTAM   VERIFIED

SECTION : 1. CHASE-II

SUB-SECTIONS	Birmingha 1/ 2/'91 POINTS [1]	Birmingha 1/ 7/'91 POINTS [2]	SUMMARY RESULTS PERCENT	ACTUAL	MAXIMUM
1. LEGAL REQUIREMENTS AND	57	133	61.7%	190	308
2. TOOLS, EQUIPMENT, FIXTURES AND	50	60	35.5%	110	310
3. MACHINERY AND PLANT	27	61	48.4%	88	182
4. CHEMICALS AND SUBSTANCES	20	20	24.7%	40	162
5. VEHICLES	60	60	48.0%	120	250
6. ENERGY	16	21	15.2%	37	244
7. HEALTH	70	70	45.2%	140	310
8. TASKS	16	16	19.0%	32	168
9. PEOPLE	28	28	28.0%	56	200
10. FEEDBACK FOR HEALTH AND SAFETY	51	63	33.9%	114	336
11. CHANGE	15	40	27.5%	55	200
12. EMERGENCIES AND SPECIAL CASES	25	50	41.7%	75	180

TOTAL MARKS: ACTUAL   435   622   1057
               MAXIMUM   1425   1425   2850
               PERCENTAGE 30.5%   43.6%   37.1%

Signed _____

Figure 6.3. *Example of CHASE II health and safety audit analysis (Copyright: Health and Safety Technology And Management ltd., 1992)*

Regular use of the system enables companies to monitor improvements or deterioration over time. For example, in Figure 6.3. a CHASE II summary table shows that for the Birmingham depot of a UK company, in some areas of health and safety management there was a significant increase in scores over the period 1 February 1991 (Column 1) to 1 July 1991 (Column 2). The average percentage score has increased from 30,5% in February to 43,6% in July whilst the scores for management of hazards from machinery and plant had risen from 27 to 61. Further breakdowns by section allows detailed scrutiny of performance in each area covered by the questions. Results can also be resented in graphical form to allow information to be communicated widely within the company. Figure 6.4 shows an example of a cascade graph for the twelve sections in CHASE II for three sequential audits conducted in January, April and July 1990. The bars show the section scores for each audit period and allow changes in scores to be identified quickly. CHASE modules include audits of health and safety, environmental management, construction project safety and hazardous substances management.

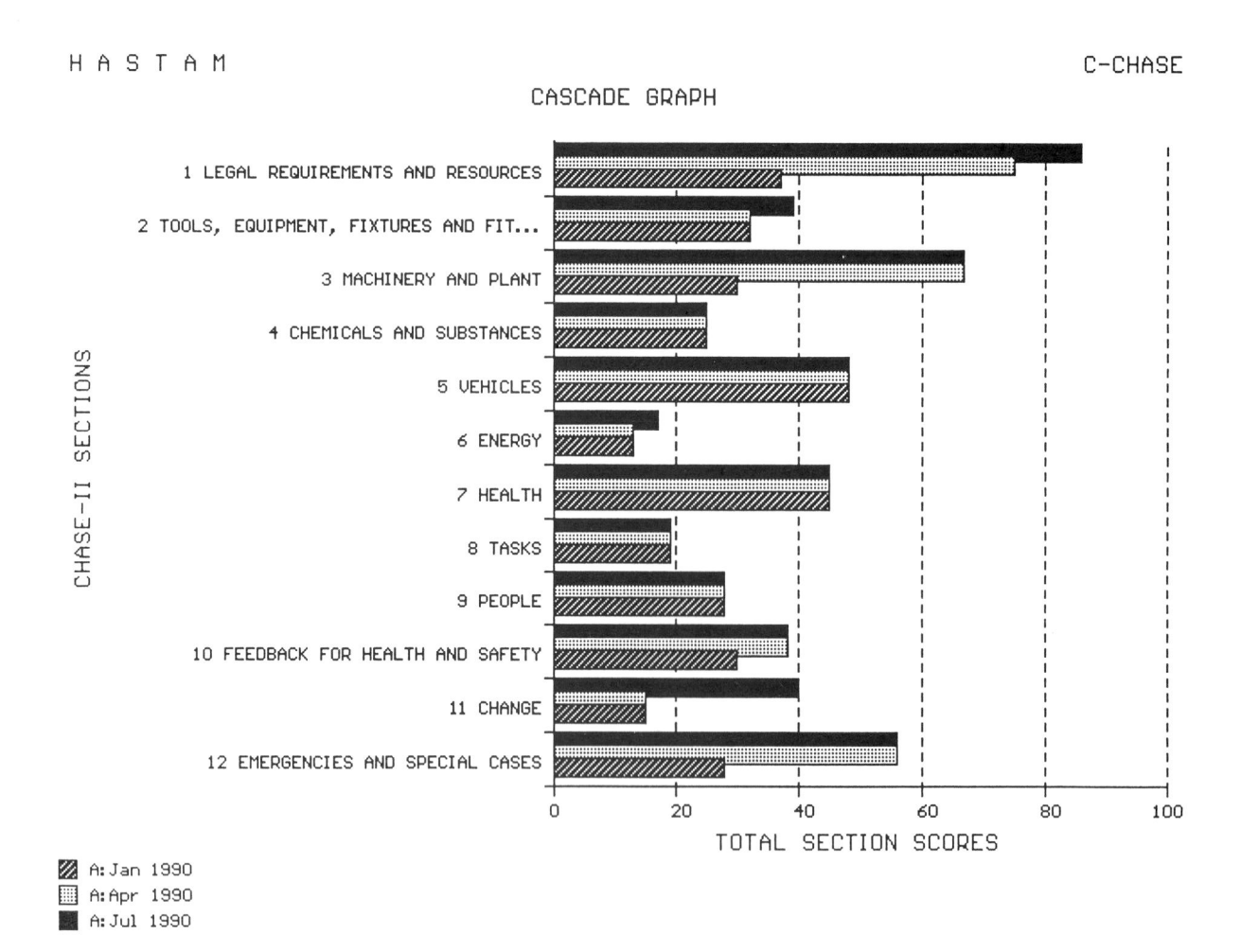

Figure 6.4. **CHASE II health and safety audit performance chart. (Copyright: Health and Safety Technology And Management Ltd., 1992)**

Environmental audits are similar to health and safety audits. The methods of environmental auditing parallel those used in health and safety, and indeed in some instances environmental issues are dealt with as part of wider health and safety audits. A summary check-list based on the recommendations made by the Confederation of British Industry is shown in Figure 6.5.

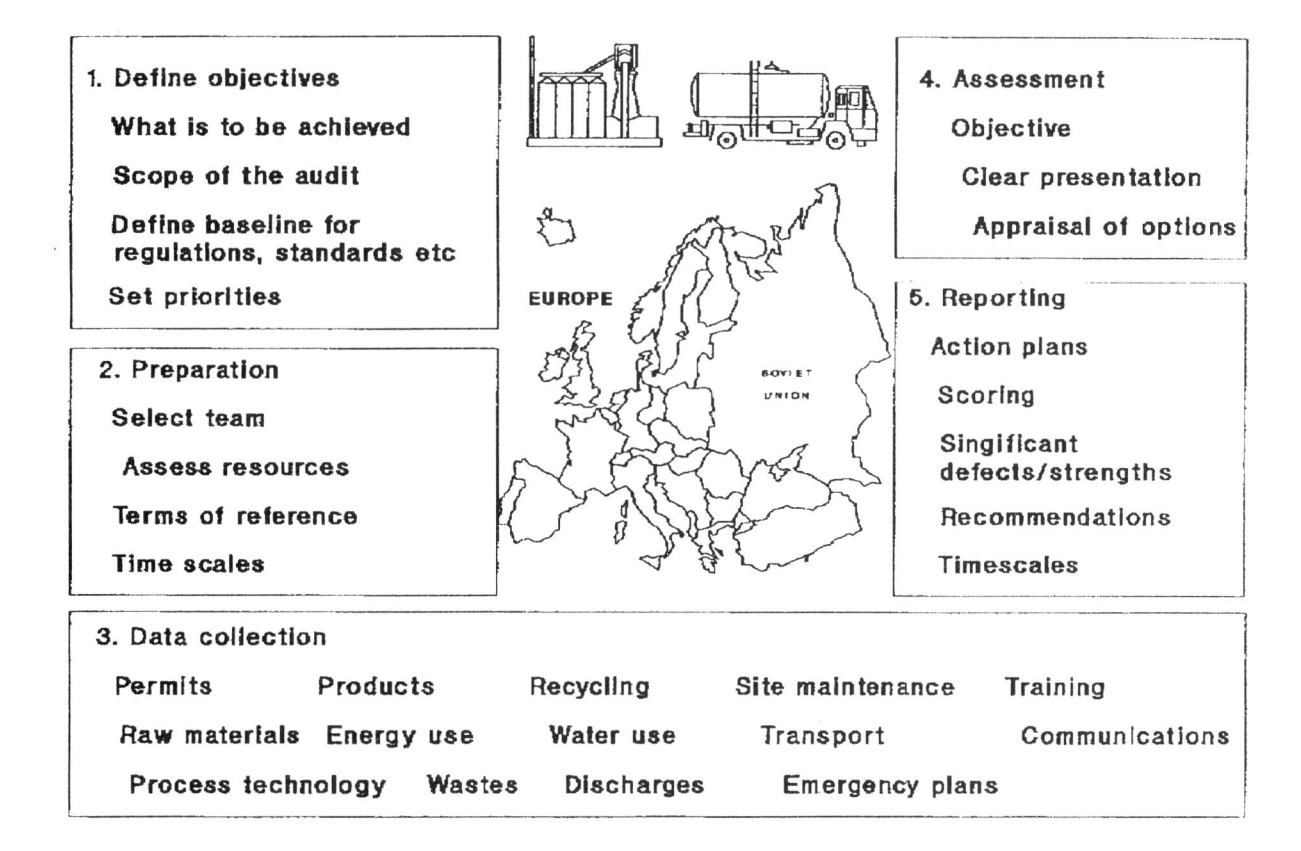

1. Define objectives		4. Assessment
What is to be achieved		Objective
Scope of the audit		Clear presentation
Define baseline for regulations, standards etc		Appraisal of options
Set priorities	EUROPE	5. Reporting
2. Preparation		Action plans
Select team		Scoring
Assess resources		Significant defects/strengths
Terms of reference		Recommendations
Time scales		Timescales

3. Data collection				
Permits	Products	Recycling	Site maintenance	Training
Raw materials	Energy use	Water use	Transport	Communications
Process technology	Wastes	Discharges	Emergency plans	

Figure 6.5. *Environmental audit action plan*

The development of auditing methods has been given significant impetus following the European Commission proposals to introduce an Environmental Auditing scheme for industry throughout the EEC. Several proprietary methods have already been developed including Environment-CHASE (14) and COURSAFE.

6.3. THEMATIC ASSESSMENT METHODS

Thematic assessment methods focus upon specific stages or a combination of stages in the manufacturing process, workplace factors and their consequences. Assessment may be carried out by an external assessor or by an internal assessor or team. In Appendix II we have included a manual of key questions which can be used at company level as a tool to identify, evaluate and control the problems. The manual covers all of the common work environment and environment factors, problems related to work organisation and psycho-social conditions at work.

Assessment of Hazards and Risk associated with operations or facilities

Assessments aimed at identifying, evaluating and controlling hazards to health, safety and the environment cover most aspects of the manufacturing process from work organisation, management systems; the hazards themselves including potential failures, emissions and chemical, physical and biological factors; and the impact or projected effects on health and safety or the environment. Hazards may be in the form of combinations of factors in circumstances which then give rise to an adverse effect.

A basic distinction must be drawn between the concepts of hazard and risk. A hazard is an aspect of an activity that has the capacity to cause harm. Risk on the other hand is an assessment of the probability that the hazard will in fact cause harm.

Within an organisation, there may be several ways in which hazards are identified including inspection, discussions with operators and local residents or audits. Workplace inspections are undertaken with the aim of identifying potential or actual hazards and initiating remedial action to control these hazards. These may be performed by managers, supervisors or advisers on a regular basis using check-lists or inspection proformas. Group discussions about operations or proposed operations may be valuable part of the hazard identification process. Involvement of the workers engaged in the task is an essential aspect of identifying potential problems. Audits, as discussed previously, may also identify potential hazards.

Once a hazard is identified, the problem may be investigated in detail. The level of assessment will clearly depend on the type and scale of the problem being addressed. For straightforward problems the solution may be immediately apparent and action instigated. Where problems are more complex or fundamental, more structured systematic investigation is usually required. There are a large range of methods that have been developed to assess hazards and quantify risks. At its simplest, a listing of all hazards identified may be drawn up and rated according to the likely frequency, severity, probability (risk) and maximum possible damage or loss (MPL). Numerical formula can then be developed to give overall rating scores for each hazard enabling priorities for control to be established. Task or Job Safety Analysis (JSA) (15) is an accident prevention technique that is applied in the development of safe systems of work using the following stages:

- the task or job is broken down into discrete stages and each one is selected in turn.
- each stage is critically observed and examined to determine the risk of an accident.
- control measures are developed.
- Safe systems of work and job safety instructions are written and installed.
- system are maintained, monitored and reviewed regularly.

More sophisticated techniques are available to aid evaluation of hazards and risks. Fault tree analysis for example is a technique that can be used after an accident or incident to trace back through the chronological sequence of events in order to identify the causes and effects that have contributed to the problem. Hazard And Operability Studies (HAZOP) (16) may be applied to existing or planned facilities or installations to assess the hazard potential from maloperation or failure of individual components of the system and then to project the consequences for the facility as a whole. This technique is applied by a team of specialists from a wide range of disciplines who collect and evaluate data on the process, possible failures, and their consequences. Information may be obtained using a wide variety of methods, for example gas dispersion modelling to predict the spread and likely impact of gas releases. There are a large range of other techniques that may be used in identifying and assessing hazards in the workplace and the environment including Techniques of Operations Review which is an analytical or tracing system that is used by system designers and managers to examine the underlying and contributory factors that may contribute to failures; Gross Hazard Analysis which is used in the early design stages and considers the hazards arising from the total system; Classification of risks and risk ranking.

Assessment of Specific Hazards Arising from Production Operations

The first important elements of a manufacturing operation, are the necessary tools, equipment, work areas and substances which are required for production, operation and maintenance activities. In a factory environment, this will be all those aspects of the operation that are contained or used in production areas, storage, distribution etc. In an office environment, the equivalents would be desks, typewriters, store rooms, ventilation plant, cleaning and other substances such as solvents. At this level, assessments are widely used to identify particular aspects which constitute avoidable or serious risks to health and safety.

Hazardous substances are found in all working environments. These may include toxic chemicals, corrosives, fine dusts, and bacteria. They may be present because they are used directly in manufacturing as raw materials, intermediates or products or alternatively they be present due to contamination, process failures, unwanted side reactions, wastes, secondary chemical reactions taking place in the workplace environment or degradation of materials used in the building or in systems. Assessments may be performed in existing facilities in order to identify potential hazards to health, or may be applied during the design stages. Identification of a problem associated with hazardous materials may be identified from complaints or obvious signs such as visible fumes, dusts or information about substances such as labels. In other cases problems may be less readily apparent with no clear evidence of immediate effects on health comfort or visible signs of contamination or exposure. For this reason assessments should be undertaken for all substances used and for all operations involving exposure to substances or materials. In the UK, the Control of Substances Hazardous to Health Regulations

1988 (COSHH) require that assessments are undertaken whenever substances are used or may be present that are toxic, harmful, corrosive or irritant, or have been assigned Occupational Exposure Standards or which have delayed or chronic affects on health. The Approved Code of Practice linked to the Regulations states that "The Purpose of the Assessment is to enable a valid decision to be made about the measures necessary to control substances hazardous to health arising from any work. It also enables the employer to demonstrate readily, both to himself and other persons, that all the factors pertinent to the work have been considered, and that informed and valid judgement has been reached about the risks, the steps which need to be taken in order to achieve and maintain adequate control, the need for monitoring exposure at the workplace and the need for health surveillance". Assessments require firstly that substances and operations are identified, secondly that the hazards associated with each substance are identified, thirdly that the risks of exposure for individuals are assessed and finally that recommendations are put forward on measures necessary to achieve effective controls that reduce risks to health. Risks to health may be assessed for example by using the following check-list:

1. Obtain information about substances by observation and investigation and consider:

- Where and in what circumstances substances are used, handled, generated, released etc.
- What happens to them in use - is their form changed (eg solids reduced to dusts by machining)? Identify places, eg handling departments, storage areas, transport;
- What people are doing; what might they do;
- What measures are currently taken to control exposure and to check on the effectiveness and use of those measures;
- Who will be affected (eg employees, employers, contractors, public);

2. If exposure is liable to occur:

- is it likely some of the substances will be breathed in?
- is it likely to be swallowed following contamination of fingers, clothing etc?
- is it likely to cause skin contamination or be absorbed through the skin?
- is it reasonably foreseeable that an accidental leakage, spill or discharge could occur (eg, through breakdowns of the plant or control measures or operators mistakes)?

3. Reach conclusions about people's exposure: who, under what circumstances, the length of time they are or could be exposed for, the amount they are exposed to, and how likely exposure is to occur. Combine this with knowledge about the potential of the substance for causing harm (ie its hazard) to reach conclusions about the risks from exposure.

Hazards arising from machinery may be identified through inspections, tests, observations, records of accidents etc. The assessment procedure should be very similar to that employed for hazardous substances but with its focus on physical hazards such as trapping, severance, impact etc.

Other types of assessment may be used to examine the effects of exposure of operators to factors that may have adverse consequences on health, safety, comfort and effectiveness in the context of their working environment and particularly their interaction with equipment used in work activities. Such ergonomic assessments cover a very wide and varied range of circumstances and may be applied in the study of existing workplaces, or in the design of new facilities and work organisation/management systems. Ergonomic assessment may also address aspects of machinery and hazardous substances assessments considered above.

Assessment of Specific Workplace or Environmental Factors

As can be seen from Figure 6.1, manufacturing operations may give rise to a variety of workplace and environmental factors such as psychological load, noise, gases, dusts etc. These factors may have already been identified or considered as part of detailed thematic assessments of machinery or hazardous substances considered in the assessments described above. There will be circumstances, however, where they are considered in isolation. For example, a noisy factory environment may be caused by the combined effects of noise and vibration emitted from a large number of machines, transport devices, people etc. Therefore, the type of assessment that is conducted in investigating a noise problem, takes as its starting point the characteristics and distribution of noise within the environment, and then examines where the noise is originating from and may assess its possible consequences for health.

Assessments which take workplace or environmental factors as their focus make use of wide variety of measuring, monitoring, modelling and prediction techniques. In many cases companies will require specialist advice on the selection, operation and interpretation of results of monitoring surveys.

Assessment of the Consequences of Exposure to Workplace or Environmental Factors

As has been indicated in Figure 6.1, the consequences of exposure to workplace or environmental factors may be assessed either through the techniques of hazard and risk assessment previously discussed above, or more specifically through assessments orientated towards the effects on health, safety or the environment. Environmental effects are addressed through the techniques of environmental impact assessment which is largely applied in the design stages of projects as a means of identifying potential impacts on the environment so that the best design option can be selected and controls built into the development. This technique could also be used for existing installations and it likely that this type of assessment will be increasingly used with the emergence of public pressures to clean-up industry. The equivalent in workplace health and safety are those techniques which examine the impact of exposure to workplace environmental factors on health and safety. The starting point for these types of assessments is the existence or forecasts of the incidence of disease, accidents and other indicators of health impact such as body burdens, biological effects etc. From knowledge of the effects on health, it is then possible to identify potential options for reducing risks to health.

7. Options for describing solutions

This section of the report reviews issues connected to the implementation of the solutions that are identified from the results of an assessment in particular how information can be communicated to designers/suppliers.

The outcome of an assessment process will be a recommendation to do something or in some cases to do nothing. In situations where solutions are proposed, these may require further inputs from technical experts, advisers and technicians. Design of control measures, changes in processes or work methods may involve additional expertise to that used in the assessment. This raises the issue of communication. The results of the assessment and its recommendations should be made available to those who will responsible for designing and then implementing the chosen solution. Frequently, problems are encountered where the requirements of the solution are not adequately explained or understood by suppliers, designers, manufacturers etc.

The required functional specifications of the solution can be described in qualitative or quantitative terms. It is also possible to describe the solution in terms of its function or as technical specifications as illustrated by the following example of a simple noise problem associated with a wood planning machine.

	1. FUNCTION OF THE SOLUTION	2. TECHNICAL SOLUTION
QUALITATIVE TERMS	* No risk of hearing impairment * Conversation must be possible * No impact to ergonomics	* The planner machine must be enclosured * Sound traps in operation openings
QUANTITATIVE TERMS	* 80 dB(A) must not be exceeded * Draught from L.E. ventilation beneeth 0,25 m/sec.	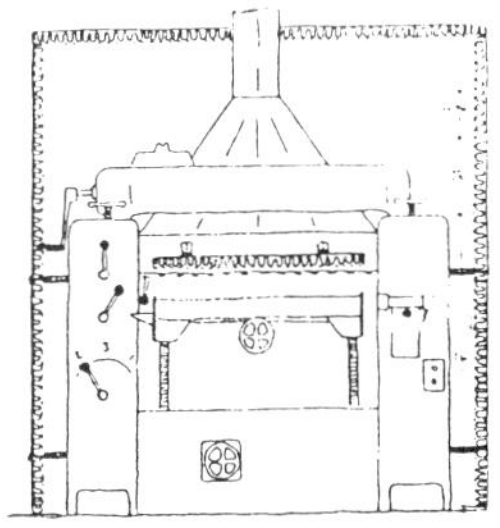

Fig. 7.1. Description of demands to the technical solution and its function, ex. from noise mitigation in a joiner's workshop: *Planning machine.*

The example in Figure 7.1. the noise mitigation of a planing machine is an illustration of a methodical approach. With this example it is not being said, that noise enclosure is the best way to mitigate noise but other preventive measures could be possible such as a change of the part of the machinery which generates noise, i.e. change of velocity and/or the cutting tool. The key point is that specific work environment and environment solution should be based on the description of demands and requirements to the solution. This is the only way to control implementation of a solution. From the workers experience this is badly needed.

In the context of planning new buildings, alterations and implementation of new technology, this is also a crucial point, because it denotes different ways to translate user language into the language of the technicians and designers. And this is a key problem in planning processes.

However, at this point it must be emphasized that this approach not only applies to simple technical work environment problems, it is also applies when the work environment problem is complex, i.e. the development of new systems of work organization as an answer to problems associated with monotonous operations.

By this it is emphasized that the Figure 7.1. illustrates a methodical approach, and it is obvious that the different categories of demands have their own advantages in accordance to the purpose: control of the solution, expression of expectations, detailed information so misunderstandings are avoided and finally the degree of freedom of the designers to select solutions. (4)(7)(17)

In the following these four perspectives on specifying the demands of a solution will be examined and illustrated.

7.1. THE FUNCTION OF THE SOLUTION

Qualitative demands

This is the most common way in which the company and the user describe the requirements of the solution to a problem. The language is typically that of the company and the operators: i.e. "The solution must conform to relevant legislation", "We want the best possible solution", "We want good quality air in the breathing zone", "We need a flexible system of operation". Such qualitative expressions clearly reflect the outcome of the workplace assessment as well as the needs and expectations of the management and the operators.

Open-ended, easily misunderstood or imprecise expressions such as these are bound to cause confusion and possibly failure to meet expectations. While it is very important to express the desires of the managers and workers in a basic way, careful consideration should be given to the way in which qualitative requirements are expressed. One answer is to ensure that the designer fully understands demands and needs of the company and the users, possibly through discussions with workers, managers, assessors etc. They may be encouraged to participate in the group responsible for coordinating the assessment itself, and it must be emphasized that the users are "specialists" in describing qualitative demands and needs.

Quantitative demands

The description of the work environment solution in quantitative terms is also referred to as performance or technical specifications. Description of these demands requires specialized knowledge and experience because these specifications must be designed to fulfil the demands and needs of the company and the users.

Technical specifications may focus on the performance characteristics of the source, the preventive measures or the exposure conditions, as shown in Figure 7.2. (18)(19)

The source: "Evaporation must not exceed 2 gr. pr. sec."

The measure: "Eshausted volume of air must be at least 1.000 m^3/h

The exposure: "Air concentration in breathing zone must not exceed 25 ppm."

Fig. 7.2. Description of technical specifications with the focus on the source, the preventive measures or the exposure conditions.

In this illustration the technical specifications relate to a very simple work environment problem: a painting operation involving organic solvents. Technical specifications can be described in the context of any work environment or external environmental problem such as noise, ergonomics, toxic factors, or air quality.

Where exposure or environmental standards exist (such as for noise, water or atmospheric contamination), there is a tendency to use these as technical specifications. In some cases performance criteria may be expressed as a proportion of the exposure standard (i.e. % of TLV or OES). In setting such specifications, companies and their consultants should be aware of the difficulties which may be encountered in achieving such levels. Measurement may also be complex and expensive. An example from practice is given in Figure 7.3.:

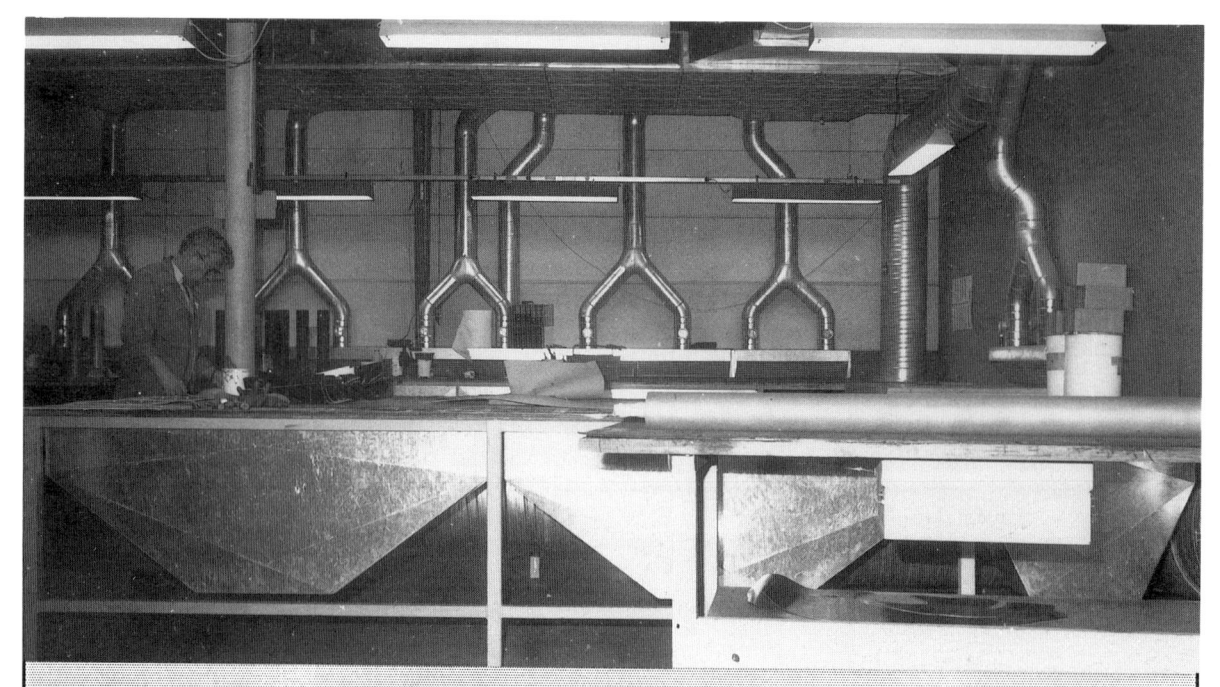

In a company which vulcanize rubber by gluing an uncertainty concerning the supplier's offer of a Local Exhaust Ventilation resulted in technical specifications:

1. **Aimed at the measure:**

a. The reference condition of the exhaust ventilation system must be described in exhausted volumes.

b. Exhausted volumes must be specified at each workstation

c. Measurement points must be shown

d. A 15% measurement uncertainty ... will be accepted

e. The system must be delivered including a report on measurements

f. A complete instruction manual covering of operation and maintenance must be included

2. **Aimed at the exposure conditions**

a. Operators exposure must not exceed 0,25 x TLV, during the gluing of 14 normal rubber articles

b. Draught must not exceed 0,25 m/sec at work stations

c. Noise from the LEV must not exceed 65 dB(A) measured at the work stations

Fig. 7.3. Specifications on a LOCAL EXHAUST ventilation system in the suppliers contract.

7.2 THE TECHNICAL SOLUTION

Qualitative demands

The solution to a workplace or environmental problem can be described in terms of specific technical requirements. In general this has to do with the level at which the problem is expected to be solved. One very robust solution is to eliminate the problem of source by a change in the manufacturing process, other solutions may be based on acceptance of the problem of source and efforts will be made to hinder the spread and exposure. In specific the work to do is to prioritise among different preventive methods and the overall preventive methods are: (18)

Eliminate the problem source
1. Implementation of a new technical system
2. Technical change in existing manufacturing system, i.e. substitution

Hinder the spread
3. Enclosure of source
4. Hinder the spread

Hinder the exposure
5. Enclosure or removal of people
6. Change of work patterns
7. Personal protection equip.

Specific specialized knowledge is often required to ensure that the chosen methods of control are realistic. For example, in Denmark, a computerised toxic substances substitution system called SUBFAC has been developed to aid selection of safer alternatives for process materials.

Description of solutions in terms of qualitative demands may also usefully include the previous experiences of the company and users. Operation experience and exposure experience are also important inputs to the design of solutions, as shown in the following example:

```
2.    ...
3.    The LEV must be available to every workstation in the
      glueing section
4.    The workstation where glue and hardener is mixed,
      stored and waste is handled must be included
5.    The system should be easy to clean and maintain
6.    The LEV must not hinder normal operation
7.    The LEV must operate with as low volumes of air as
      possible
8.    Enclosures must be used wherever practicable
9.    ...
```

Fig. 7.4. *Ex.: Qualitative demands for a local exhaust ventilation system*

In the above example, qualitative statements are used not to give complete information about the requirements of the solution, but to express the demands and expectations of the company and the users. These demands and expectations are controlable.

Quantitative demands

Quantitative demands are the actual technical and performance specifications that a solution is expected to meet.

Detailed specification in this way enables companies to evaluate the probable effectiveness of proposed solution prior to contract, i.e. "the point of no return".

Experienced gained through mock-up studies, pilot studies or scale trials (especially full-scale or 1:1 tests) can be particularly valuable in giving detailed design information. Visits to other sites where the solution has already been used are another way of gathering quantitative information that can then be used as a basis for specification of solutions.

This type information can be helpful as it allows users to examine the proposed solution and see how it works, before the full solution is implemented.

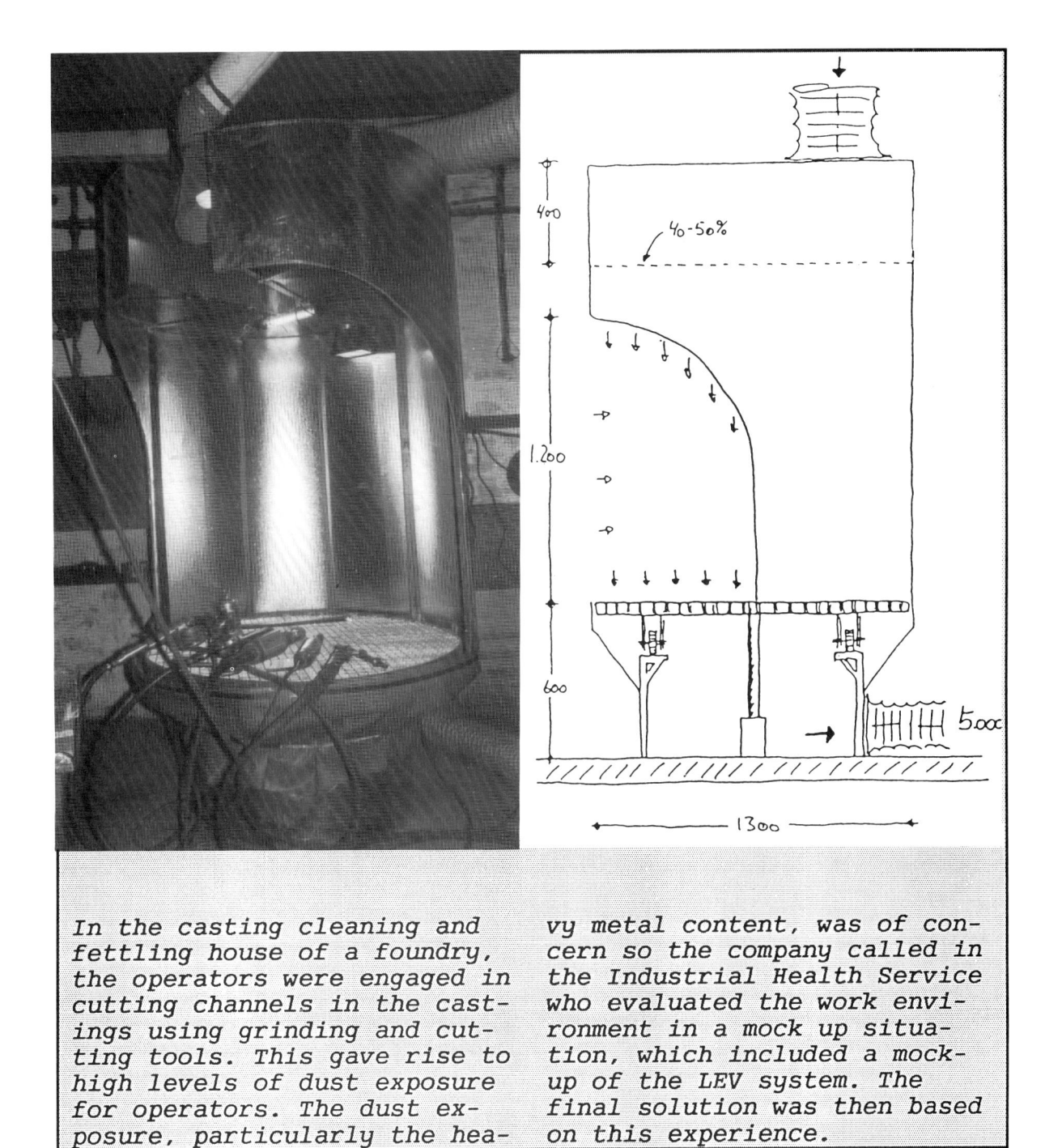

In the casting cleaning and fettling house of a foundry, the operators were engaged in cutting channels in the castings using grinding and cutting tools. This gave rise to high levels of dust exposure for operators. The dust exposure, particularly the heavy metal content, was of concern so the company called in the Industrial Health Service who evaluated the work environment in a mock up situation, which included a mock-up of the LEV system. The final solution was then based on this experience.

Fig. 7.5. Construction of mock-up: draft grinding bench at a foundry.

8. Practical experience - 5 case studies.

The previous section contains descriptions of some important fundamental concepts and methods in connection with evaluation of work environment and the general environment in and around factories. The control theme has been a description of the sequence of assessment activities, the organisational framework and the assessment activities, including involvement of the work force, and finaly the all important concrete description of assessment methods and methods for describing preventative solutions.

It has been important to point out the possibilities for involving the work force in the assessment activities. In this final section, practical experiences from 2 English and 3 Danish factories. The examples describe the experiences from strategic and thematic assessment of work environment and environmental problems both with regard to existing production and with regard to planning of new production. In this way the examples serve as an illustration of the report's recommendations for works' organisation with regard to work environment and environmental condition, and the recommendations for methods where problems are investigated and solutions carried out.

8.1 NILPETER A/S: AUTHORITARIAN MANAGEMENT METHODS SHOULD BE BROKEN DOWN IN THE PLANNING OF A NEW FACTORY WITH OPEN LAY-OUT, DK.

The machine works Nilpeter A/S decided, in 1986, to build a new factory where the factory design and fittings should support the wish for a breaking down of levels in the authoritarian management system and in this way improve collaboration. The basic requirements were that the factory should be built on an open lay-out style plan, and that it should be clean. Requirements for the work environment played an important role but only as a part of a general desire to improve the company's industrial relations, for example, with regard to increased influence of work force concerning recruiting and purchase of new machinery, interior design of ones own work place and personnel policy factors such as cantine agreements, holidays and sports facilities. The work environment has been greatly improved even though systematic assessment and evaluation methods have not been used.

Keywords: Planning of new factory, project coordination, formulation of general building needs and detailed work environment needs, involvement of users.

Introduction to Nilpeter A/S and the building plans

The machine works Nilpeter A/S, which manufactores label printing machines, is based in Slagelse on Zealand and has around 200 employees. The company is divided into departments for administration and sales, and service and production. The production department employs 180 mostly skilled workers, 30% of whom are on shift-work. The company's turn-over is around 200 million Dkr. 90% of production is exported.

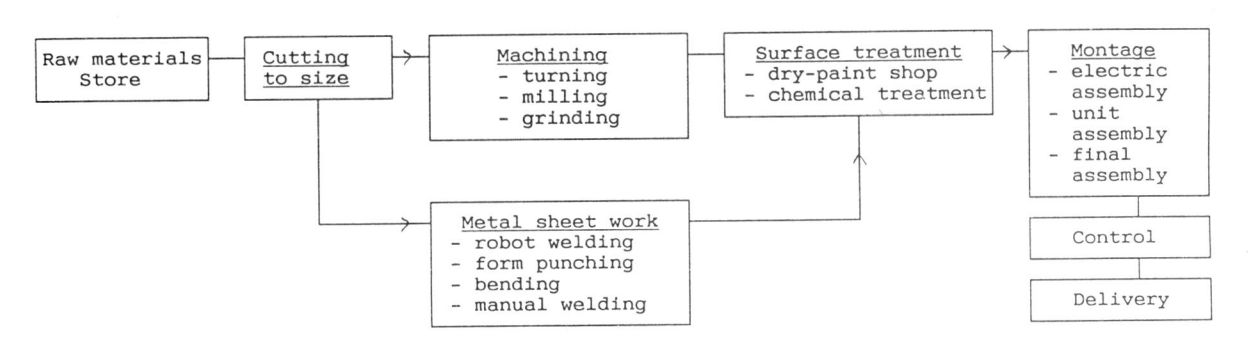

```
┌──────────┐  ┌────────┐   ┌──────────────┐   ┌──────────────────┐   ┌──────────────┐
│Raw       │  │Cutting │   │Machining     │   │Surface treatment │   │Montage       │
│materials ├─▶│to size ├──▶│- turning     ├──▶│- dry-paint shop  ├──▶│- electric    │
│Store     │  │        │   │- milling     │   │- chemical        │   │  assembly    │
└──────────┘  └───┬────┘   │- grinding    │   │  treatment       │   │- unit        │
                  │        └──────────────┘   └──────────────────┘   │  assembly    │
                  │                                  ▲               │- final       │
                  │        ┌──────────────────┐      │               │  assembly    │
                  │        │Metal sheet work  │      │               └──────┬───────┘
                  └───────▶│- robot welding   ├──────┘                      │
                           │- form punching   │                      ┌──────▼───────┐
                           │- bending         │                      │Control       │
                           │- manual welding  │                      └──────┬───────┘
                           └──────────────────┘                             │
                                                                     ┌──────▼───────┐
                                                                     │Delivery      │
                                                                     └──────────────┘
```

Fig. 8.1.1. *The production line at Nilpeter A/S*

Production can be divided into functions, typical for metal working industries, for example sawing/buffing, form punching, welding, surface treatment and assembly. This type of industry is traditionally plagued by work environment problems such as aerosols, humidity and smells from turning machines, painting shop and other surface treatment shops and generally high noise levels and hard physical work. In the external general environment the related problems of noise, exhaust air, and sorting of waste materials exist.

Background for the plans for building "Factory P4" on an open lay-out plan

In 1981 the management reacks on several years of poor frofits and firing of employees, by forming an internal works group to analyse the problems. The problems were partly technical, for example, with respect to construction and quality, but also managerial and to do with industrial relations. The management system was authoritarian: the atmosphere was very formal and a piece work payment system ensured control over the work done. In the words of the head of production: "We had a system which encouraged egotism and there were no common goals". The Steering Group was made up of 4 members from the management and 4 workers. The group's work principle was "speak freely, reference can only be made where the parties are in agreement". The Steering Group agreed on replacing the piece work system with a bonus system, where imporved productivity was rewarded with extra pay. This resulted in "going from confrontation to collaboration", and productivity rose by 21,2% in 1982. In 1986 the bonus system was changed to a profit sharing agreement, which at the end of the '80s worked out to be an extra months salary per year per head.

Rising demand meant that in 1985 Nilpeter A/S needed to expand and build, in the first case, a "Factory P3" 1250 m^2 in area and with a manpower of 25. Most notable about this factory was the open lay-out, that is to say that no part of the production was seperated off. Not even the administrative staff had a seperate room. Another very notable point was the cleanliness of the factory, where floors, walls, machines, and installations were painted white. The open lay-out and the white, clean factory come from a common wish from the Work's Steering Group. An open lay-out had to bring improvements for the work environment, and the idea was that collaboration should be strengthened and supported by the lay-out. The psychological and physical layers were to be broken down, and the works should be able to attract skilled labour. Inspiration came from works visits which the Steering Group paid to Danish works with open lay-out and very clean German factories.

3 months after start-up of "P3" yet another expansion was called for. In May 1986 it was decided to build "Factory P4".

Organisational framework for the planning of "Factory P4"

An engineer was recruited to the Technical production department to plan and coordinate in connection with Factory P4. It became this engineers responsibility to work together with the factory's boss and ensure smooth progress in the proceedings. The main characters were:

- The company/project coordinators were responsible for applying for building permission, planning of interior and the technical production equipment, contacting building firms and machine suppliers, and involvement of the work force. The work's technical production department is a key element here.

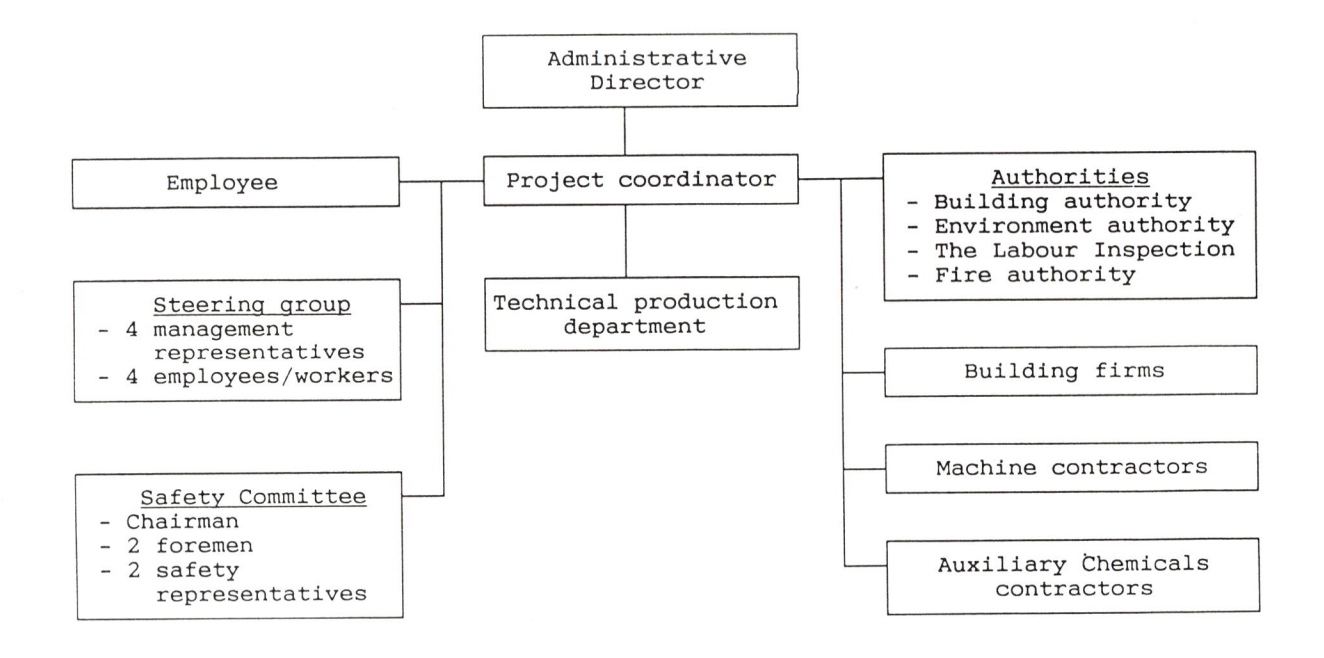

Fig. 8.1.2. The organisational structure around the planning of "Factory P4".

- The building firm was given the job of planning the building, as well as the construction work itself. The planning of the building included making proposals,

planning submission of proposals for approval by the authorities, and drawing up the building plans themselves.
- <u>The work force</u> is involved in several ways. The Steering Group is central to the whole project and with regular meetings (every 14 days) the members are informed about progress. The Health and Safety Committee is asked to make suggestions concerning the plans and finaly the work force is asked their opinion, individually or in groups, about the plans for interior design of the factory with regard to internal transport and the individual's work place.

The point of outset for the building project is a questionnaire on Main wishes and requirements for the new factory. The wish was for a clean open lay-out factory with logical internal transport routes. Technological improvements should be implemented in both production (CNC turning machines and robot-welders) and the technical departments (CAD/CAM/DNC). The factory should be built for 120 employees since this was regarded as the ideal size. From "P3" it was known that the building should be 6000 m^2. The buildings budget, including equipment and fittings, was 35 million Dkr.

These wishes and requirements were then to be converted into drawings and descriptions of the building and its interior design. Detailed description of the interior design and fittings is important with regard to the factory's future work environment. These activities can, to a certain extent, be seen as independent of the building's planning and are started relatively late in the procedure, actually after construction has started.

Fig. 8.1.3. *The open lay-out style plan includes the cantine. The department of administration and technical planning is at second floor, still in open lay-out.*

```
                Nilpeter stipulates wishes and requirements
                -    ground area: 6000 m², 120 employees
                -    total budget: Dkr. 35 mill.
                -    open lay-out
                -    clean work environment
                -    latest/new technology to be purchased
                                    ↓
May  1986       Building firm makes proposals
                                    ↓
                Nilpeter seeks planning permission
                                    ↓
                Building firm plans the building
                                    ↓
Nov. 1986       Construction work begins
                                    ↓
                Nilpeter plans the interior
                -    suggestions concerning interior
                -    involvement of work force
                -    formulation of noise control and ventila-
                     tion needs
                -    noise control and painting of own machines
                -    purchase of latest technology
                                    ↓
                Building firm finalises permission agreements
                with the authorities
                                    ↓
Aug. 1987       Factory start-up at "P4"
```

Fig. 8.1.4. Essential dates concerning main planning activities for "Factory P4"

Planning of the future work environment

An essential common goal for the management and the work force was that industrial relations and collaboration should be improved in the new factory. The open lay-out was an important part of this effort to break down barriers and improvement of the work environment went hand in hand with this. The criteria for the new factory's work environment were not only legal requirements, but also those essential for the open-plan lay-out, and the work environment activities were simply handled as part of the improved industrial relations effort.

No systematic activities were used for the assessment of work environment problems in the old factory or to check the work environment in the new factory. The management's view was that there was not time for systematic analysis and assessment with, for example, check lists. The work in connection with, including the work environment into the building project, has happened independantly, on the company's own initiative and resources and without taking professional advice.

The method was, on the other hand, to build on past experience and collect ideas at meetings of the Safety Committee and

Steering Group. Some of the main problem areas were defined as follows:

- Local ventilation extraction on the turning machines to be increased to 800 m^3/h per machine.
- Noise control measures on all machines down to a max. level of 65 dB(A) 1 m from the machine.
- Establishment of a central system for distribution and treatment of coolants and lubricants.
- The so called preservation plant to be isolated and supplied with a local exhaust.
- Dry-paint and chemical treatment plants to be sectioned off (this was not done in the end).
- The internal crane-covering to be improved.
- All surfaces: floor, machines and equipment to be painted white.

These and other problem areas were singled out and coordinated by the project coordinator. The method for keeping a record of decisions was partly notes from meetings, but more especially a model of the factory on a scale 1:250: <u>The Modulex-model</u>. This was built and rebuilt 3 times and was the model that the workers, singly and in groups, were asked to make comments on.

The formulation of what exactly the problem areas were resulted in, for example, being able to state maximum noise requirements to the machine suppliers. It also resulted in a rebuilding of the turning machines from the old factory, with sectioning-off, noise control and painting.

Fig. 8.1.5. **Turning machines were noise controlled and all surfaces painted white.**

Fig. 8.1.6. **Even the vacuum cleaners had to be noise controlled.**

Evaluation - 5 years later

The management and work force all agree that the work environment in the new factory has improved greatly: "We have many things we didn't have before". The project with the open lay-out was successful. As a handy expression for improved work environment and industrial relations, the management point out: days lost to sickness which has fallen from 4,5% to around 1,7% for the company and nationwide is at around 3,5%. The savings from this are around 800.000 Dkr. a year. This fall in absentecism due to sickness is brought out as an economic resource which has paid for the work environment investments with regard to rebiulding of machines etc, many times over.

The work environment problems are still there however. The open lay-out has brought with it draught problems and not everyone is satisfied with the 65 dB(A) max. noise level. For example, the production foremen feel a need for limits to there work place. Also, the operators would like to see certain processes sectioned off, for example, surface chemical treatment and the painting shop. The open lay-out has, however, been very important for the management, which regards it as the correct lay-out. This is expressed in that the open lay-out and the white surroundings force people to keep the work place clean.

Fig. 8.1.7. The foremens limitation in the central part of "Factory P4".

The management is satisfied with the course of the planning of "Factory P4", but thinks the work force should probably have been involved more. This theory is in entire agreement with that of the work force. First of all they feel they have been brought in at a much too late a stage and it is suggested that next time a follow-up group should be formed as soon as the decision to go ahead with a new building is taken should bee: At this stage the first point on the agenda collaboration conditions during the project. The employees would also like systematic tools (eg. check lists) which could help them to formulate their wishes concerning construction: "Next time we want to be better at participating in this type of procedure".

Collaboration is a keyword at the factory. It is important to point out that the lay-out alone cannot ensure good industrial relations, it is only a helping factor. The Steering Group is regarded as central to future continued good industrial relations. In their own words: "The work force still needs the possibility of speaking their minds openly but unofficially".

8.2 USER INFLUENCE ON INTRODUCTION OF NEW TECHNOLOGY AT RINGSTED DUN A/S (a Danish duvet manufacturer)

Employee's from the company's duvet-stuffing department complained to the Safety Committee of badly irritating dust problem. The local Industrial Health Service were asked to assess the problem, and they recorded high dust concentrations. This, plus the stressful monotonous nature of the work led to mechanisation of the stuffing work. The employees took part in the mechanisation introduction project group, and today think that this concrete collaboration was an important step in the environmental solution: "Collaboration is important, the rest sorts its self out".

Keywords: Thematic assessment of dust and ergonomics, purchase of new technology, involvement of employees, employee identified work environment problems.

Ringsted Dun A/S and the dust problem

Ringsted Dun A/S is based at Ringsted in Zealand and produces duvets and pillows with down filling. It is a small company with around 50 employees of whom about 40 are in production. 40% of the total produce is exported. The production line consists of 2 down and feather departments and a department where duvets and pillows are manufactured.

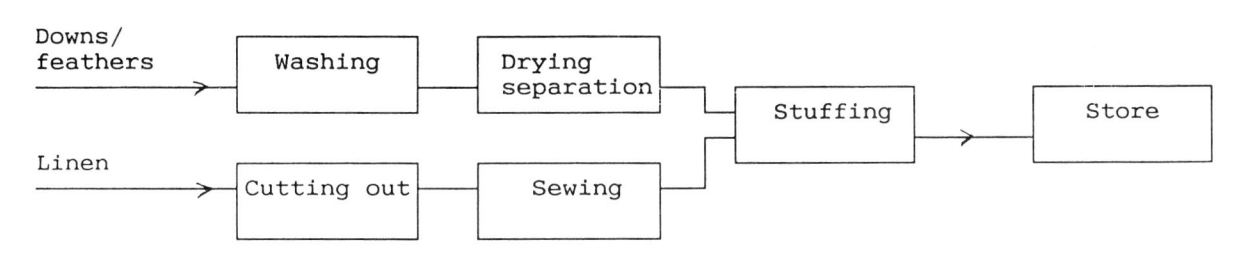

Fig. 8.2.1. **The production line at Ringsted Dun A/S**

Employees in the duvet-pillow department are typically "unskilled" women, and the work in the sewing room and stuffing room is typically monotonous work and therefore physiologically stressful. Work is paid under a piece work/bonus scheme.

The employees wanted an assessment of dust levels

Manual stuffing of duvets and pillows has always been a dusty job. In the Autumn of 1986, meanwhile, an unusually dusty raw material came on the scene and 6 employees from the stuffing room asked the Safety Committee to find a solution.

The organisational boundaries for changes in the stuffing room

Ringsted Dun A/S established a Safety Committee (SiU), and answering to that 2 Safety groups: one for preparation of feathers and down and one for manufacture of duvets and pillows.

The Committee makes decisions on work environment and health and safety problems, and in this case follow the local Industrial Health Service's investigation results through to a decision in the management on investing in a mechanical filling machine for the stuffing room. A project group was formed to coordinate this 1.5 mill. Dkr. investment.

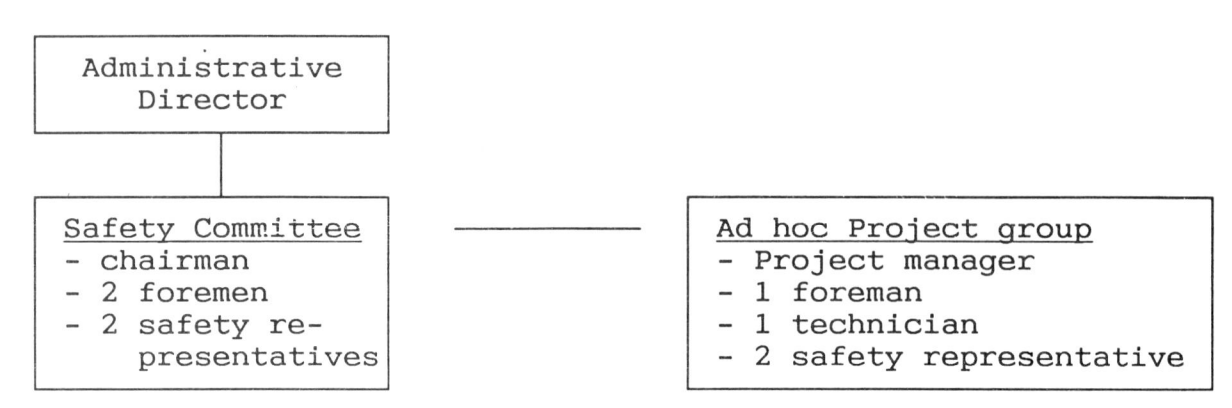

```
              Administrative
                Director
               /         \
Safety Committee        Ad hoc Project group
- chairman              - Project manager
- 2 foremen             - 1 foreman
- 2 safety re-          - 1 technician
  presentatives         - 2 safety representative
```

Fig. 8.2.2. Ringsted Dun A/S organisation with regard to work environment and changes in the stuffing department.

The project group was led by an external consultant from the company's branch society, and also included the department foreman, a technician, and the safety representative who works as an operator. It is the first time the factory has formed a project group of this kind. The reason is partly because the technical solution was too big and complicated to form a clear picture of it and partly because of the different parties involved e.g. the managements desire for increased productivity and the employees wish for a better work environment. Other contributing factors to the worker involvement were their stated interest and the managements genuine wish that the machine operators be involved in the new purchase. The Industrial Health Service could be brought in as needed and it was decided that other remedies with regard to improvement of environment and work environment should be put off until after the

```
Dust and ergonomic
assessment/investigation
         ↓
Management preparations
   for new technology
         ↓
    SiU prioritises:
project group formed
         ↓
  Planning of new
     technology
         ↓
   Approval and
    introduction
         ↓
Assessment of solutions
  w.r.t. environment
and work environment
         ↓
   Implementation
         ↓
      Control
```

Fig. 8.2.3. Steps in the assessment of techn. change.

new machinery had been set-up and tried-out. The other remedies concerned dust, noise, thermal environment, working posture and lighting. In these areas the Industrial Health Service gave advice. The final environment and work environment was controlled only with regard to the ergonomic conditions at the end of the project in the Spring of 1990.

Assessment of strain with regard to manual stuffing work

Assessment of the work environment in the stuffing department is carried out by a work environment technician and an occupational therapist from the Industrial Health Service. There are 3 central points:

1. measurement of dust,
2. recording of accupational strain and
3. recording of the employees' various irritations through a questionnaire.

The function of the questionnaire is to quickly on systematically record the employees picture of the state of the work environment. Because of this, the questionnaire is very short, consisting of 26 questions relating to work related irritants resulting from dust and physical strain from the stuffing work.

8.2.4. *The dust plaqued stuffing work*

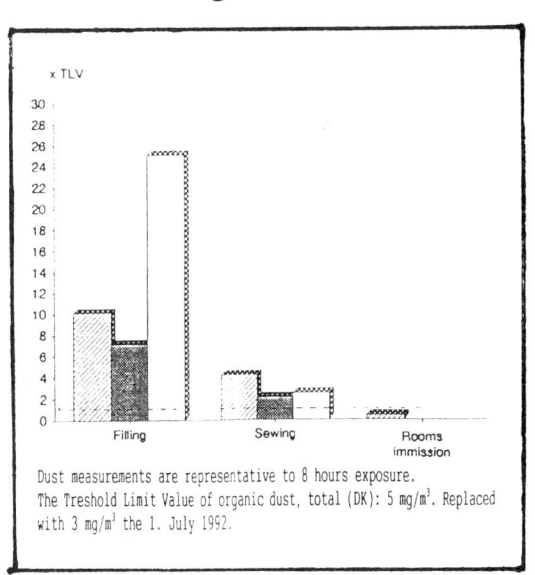

Fig. 8.2.5. *Results of dust measurement*

Dust measurements, the results from which are shown in figure 4, show that stuffing workers experience an unusually high dust-load. The high load of the sewers is mainly due to the fact that they give a hand with the stuffing work when possible. The room level, at 1 1/2 times the maximum allowable for organic dust is unacceptable. The results from the questionnaire reinforces that the work is very irritating, with complaints of, for example, itching, sneezing, coughing, muscular pains and headaches. 4 workes are sent for occupational health evaluation, permanent damage to respiratory organs is identified. Evaluation of the occupational stress concerns the weight of the duvets and pillows which have to be wielded around, work posture, range of static muscle work, the monotony of the work, and the lighting. The stress caused by the repetitious nature of the work and the pace of work is evaluated as very relevant and directly connected to pain from muscles and joints. Some of the workers need treatment from a chiropractor.

The IHS's report identifies the sources of the problems and works out a suggestion for a ventilated and heigh adjustable work place. The report suggests also better lighting, floor covering and finally, that work can be organised and led in a way such that a change from the repetitiousness of the work is made possible. The suggested solution is described with regard both for function eg. working height and extructed air quantities, and for quality of solution: what must be covered by the extracts, what must be height adjustable, etc.

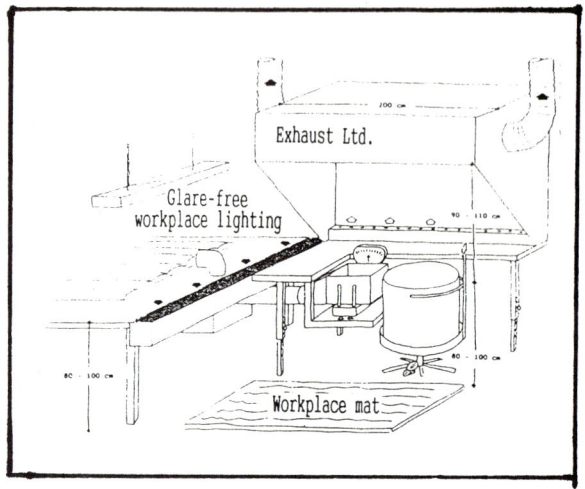

Fig. 8.2.6. Sketch of a solution.

On receiving the IHS's report and solution suggestions, the management recognised the problems with the work environment and a quick decision was made to get new technology for the stuffing room. The first assessment of the technological solution is made by a management group visiting a foreign producer in the same line of business. Experience from this visit is communicated to the operators via a report and a video. The operators feel that they should have been taken along on the visit since this would have been the best way to get information. The project group then plans the introduction of the new technology into the stuffing room. Amongst other things, position is taken with regard to the lay-out of the room from drawings, and the wishes for painting the room and need for instruction are put forward. As part of the work the project group visits other factories to build up experience. One factory had introduced similar stuffing machines and an other had done a lot with the colour and light in the work room. The group does not use check-lists but functions well with use of agenda and minutes.

After the preliminary operator experiences from the new machinery have been fathered in, the Industrial Health Service is brought in so as to evaluate the need for taking steps, and now the main focus of attention is on describing solutions. Ideas for extract air ducks are sketshed-out, including suggestions on filtering of the exhaust, and the IHS takes part in the subsequent negotiations with ventilation contractors, amongst other things it is recommended that requirements are listed, with regard to documentation of air quantities and service and maintenance instruction; that suggestions are made with regard to positioning of tables, mats and seating; and finaly it is pointed out that job rotation can improve the situation with regard to problems resulting from the repetitious fast tempo work. The work environment in the final form has been controlled only through assessment in January 1990: control measurements are not taken.

Fig. 8.2.7. *The final workstation*

Evaluation

The workers, foreman and management are satisfied with the changes in the stuffing room. Improved productivity has been achieved and the workers think that the work environment with regard to dust and physiological stress has got better. "The work today is 100 times easier", as one of the employees puts it. In the planning af the new technology, it hadn't been realised that organisation of work could also be discussed, for example, job rotation and work satisfaction, but this wasn't considered to be a failure on the side of the project group.

Among the workers and management, the most important experience gained was considered to be that collaboration is both important and beneficial. The project group was a good way to organise the work. In this case it was difficult to imagine how future work environment would look, but factory visits was a good tool.

Among shortcomings were that the completed solution has not been "checked-up" on, and that information on the operation and maintenance has been lacking in many respects. Nobody in the project group considered: "We were too taken by the positive aspects".

8.3 NOISE ASSESSMENT AND NOISE CONTROL AT PLASTMO A/S, DK

The Industrial Health Service has made an assessment of noise levels at Plastmo A/S. A noise control programme has been worked out by a noise committee and the programme anticipates that control will be carried out by experts. In one department this gives problems. Satisfactory solutions are found first after trials carried out by the employees themselves. In most cases, the employees participate in the assessment, the plan of action and the implementation of solutions. This is found to be essential by both management and employees in order to obtain a good result.

Keywords: Thematic noise assessment, assessment demanded by authorities, noise committee, different models for user participation.

Introduction to Plastmo A/S and the noise problem

Plastmo A/S is one of Denmark's largest plastics manufacturers. The factory is located in Ringsted in Zealand, and produces PVC-guttering and window frames in PVC plus PC (polycarbonate) roofing material. Plastmo A/S have around 180 employees and a turn-over of around 200 million Danish Kroner. About 60% of their produce is exported.

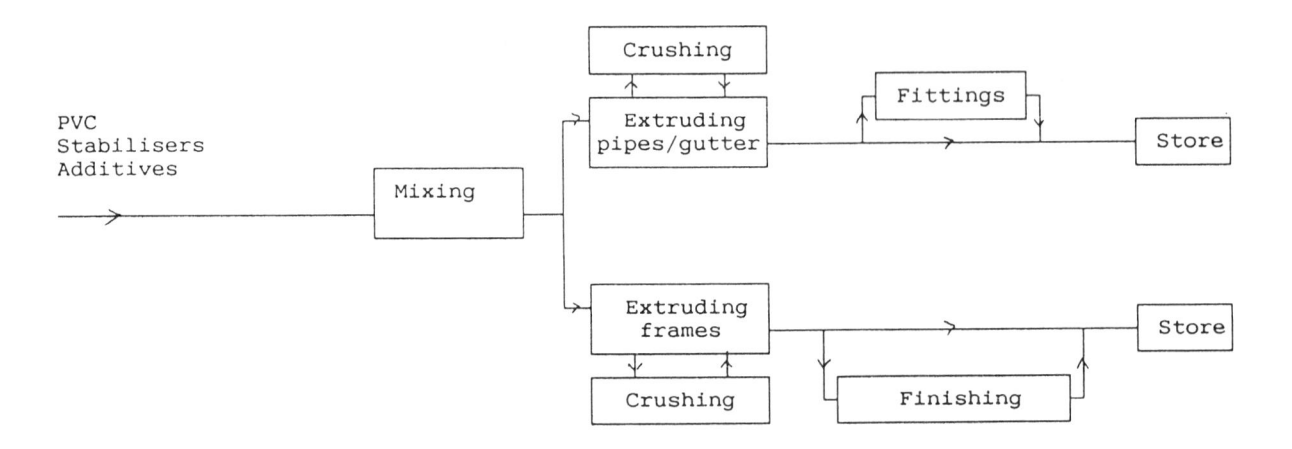

Fig. 8.3.1. Production line at Plastmo A/S

After the raw materials have been mixed, production is divided into two extruding halls: One where gutters and down-pipes are produced and fittings attached; the other where window frames and roofing material is produced with associated department for bending and cutting to size of panels: finishing. The company's work environment activity has, until now, been concentrated on controlling the development of heavy-metal impregnated dust in the mixing hall, and substituting potentially hazardous chlorinated solvents used in the gluing of attachments. Activities relating to the outdoor environment have especially concerned controlled disposal of PVC waste. This is now achieved via increased recycling and delivery of any remains to a national plant for controlled waste disposal. These activities set in motion after a public PVC-debate. In the summer of 1990 the company made its "environment plan": "Plastmo A/S will be oriented on, and live up to, relevant national and international environment regulations and intentions in both the general outdoor environment and the work environment".

The Labour Inspection demanded a noise assessment

Assessing noise in the work environment at the work stations during production was carried out in October 1989 by the local Industrial Health Service (IHS) after a request from the Safety Committee. The investigation was brought about by the local Labour Inspection, which demanded "a mapping of sound level around the factory plus a plan for bringing the noise level down". It is generally agreed at the factory that the investigation would not have been undertaken if it had not been for the Labour Inspection. In some of the departments the workers had come to accept the noise as something that simply went with the job.

The organisational boundaries for the noise assessment

The organisational boundaries for work environment work is the Safety Committee (SC) and the safety groups. There are 12 safety groups, one for each department. The safety group consists of the department's foreman and the employees' representative: the safety representative. The Safety Committee is responsible for coordination and decision making tasks in connection with work environment[1]. The company is affilliated to the "Mid-Zealand Industrial Health Service, IHS.

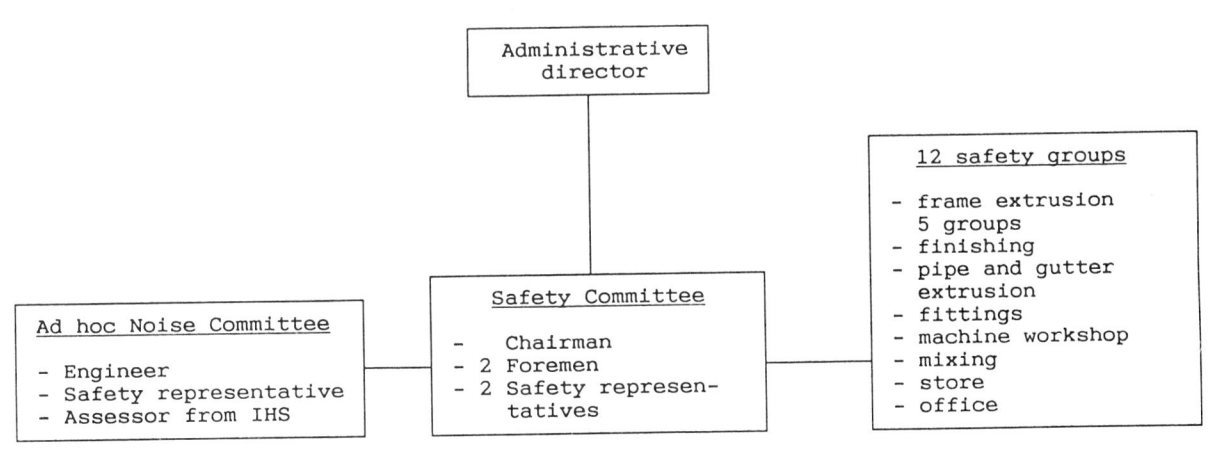

Fig. 8.3.2. *Plastmo's organisation with regard to the work environment*

---

[1] The Safety Committee is responsible for advising the company in work environment questions, to assess, to establish solutions, to inform and to check. The safety group's job is: to check that at the individual work places the work environment is reasonable, and precautionary measures are in order; to participate in planning of changes; to inform; and to report to the Safety Committee.

The noise assessment was begun in October 1989 after a decision by the Safety Committee. As part of this decision, position was also taken with regard to just where and how measurements should be taken, how the employees were to be informed and involved and a deadline set for reporting back to the Safety Committee. After the report had been processed by the Safety Committee, a noise committee was to be formed which would report, within a 4 month deadline, with its noise control programme. No budget was allocated. The noise committee consisted of a works engineer, a safety representative, and a technician from the Industrial Health Service. The Safety Committee would put the programme into action, and the Industrial Health Service would check how things stood at the end of the programme in February 1991.

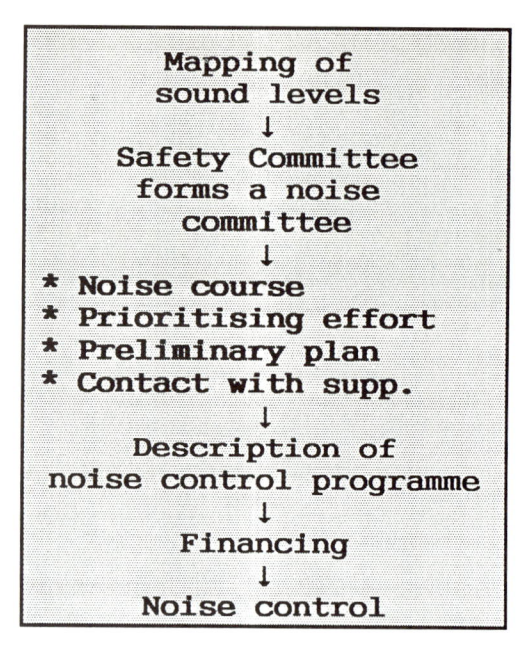

```
Mapping of
sound levels
     ↓
Safety Committee
  forms a noise
   committee
     ↓
* Noise course
* Prioritising effort
* Preliminary plan
* Contact with supp.
     ↓
  Description of
noise control programme
     ↓
   Financing
     ↓
  Noise control
```

Fig. 8.3.3. Steps in the assessment and control activities.

Noise assessment and control

Fig. 8.3.4. Interior view from extrusion department

The noise assessment is carried out by the Industrial Health Service by measuring and recording of results, and the goal has been to record the noise load at the work place. The measurements included noise dose and sound pressure level at the work place, and the results displayed together with information with regarding relation to the process, number of people exposed noise sources etc. To ensure relevant measurement results the planned measurements were gone through at a meeting with the departments foreman and safety representative. The report to the Safety Committee pointed out the total work places with a noise load of 85-90 dB(A) and work places over the 8 hour limit of 90 dB(A). It was recommended a noise committee to be formed to work out a plan of action.

The noise committee's job is to, within 4 months, carry out a noise control programme. So as to motivate and inercase insight into practical noise control, the noise committee were sent on a 1-day course, arranged by the Industrial Health Service, with teaching by experts in noise control. The course was arranged for

12 foremen and safety representatives, not only from Plastmo A/S but from industries which have similar noise problems: noise from saws, transport of materials in pipes, etc.

The noise committee <u>prioritised</u> the noise sources which were giving over 90 dB(A), together with unnecessary noise sources. See fig. 5. The 16 cut-off saws in the extrusion department were highly prioritised even though damping was not expected to bring the noise dose down. The high priority given is due

1. 16 cutt-off saws	86- 90 dB(A)
2. 3 finishing saws	88-101 dB(A)
3. The crushers	91- 99 dB(A)
4. 6 saws in the fitting dept.	94 dB(A)

Fig. 8.3.5. *Noise dose levels in prioritised areas*

to a requirement of the Labour Inspection on screening off of such saws. The company expected the noise committee to contract out the final noise reduction work to experts from firms specialising in this field. <u>Noise reduction trials</u> were therefore carried out on identical noise sources, from which contractors could <u>tender bids</u> on both single noise sources and prototypes.

| 1. prioritesed noise sources |
| 2. Noise reduction suggestions |
| 3. Evaluation of noise reduction |
| 4. Time table for implementation |
| 5. Overview of possible contractors and costs |

Fig. 8.3.6. *The contents of the noise reduction programme*

The contractors bids were evaluated from them, a noise reduction programme (5 sides) could be worked out. Total outlay was calculated to 650.000 Dkr., whilst the final cost was 335.000 Dkr. The works engineers role was as contact to the contractor, taking photographs of the noise sources, and carrying out the noise reduction programme. The safety represen tative took part in discussions and joint decision making. The Industrial Health Service carried out measurements, sketched possible solutions and gave advice with regard to contractors.

One single contract gave problems. A contractor had promised an "input reduction of 18 - 20 dB" from a double saw and check measurements showed that the operator load had only fallen from 101 to 93 dB(A), a reduction of only 8 dB. Dissatisfaction was great. The contractor explained that noise reduction would be 18 - 20 dB if the noise source was completely contained in the incapsulation In this case noise was also emitted by the section of material which stuck out of the incapsulation. The contractor in the meantime improved the solution without further ado, but the example shows that the contracted work must be described exactly when there is talk of prioritised problems, for example, with regard to interpretation and check-up conditions and methods.

The user's active involvement in the fitting department

Fig. 8.3.7. **Damped saw in the fitting department**

Fig. 8.3.8. **Systema. check-list**

1. Reduced r.p.m.
2. Change of blade: thickness, tooth-type
3. Speed of feeding "job" through
4. Better grip on the "job"
5. Air-guiding plates by the saw
6. Absorption in the saw box
7. Enclosing the saw
8. Setting up of screens
9. Reduction of room reverberation
10. Reduction of time spent at saw
11. Greater distance between operator and saw
12. Ear protection

Reduction of noise from the saws in the fitting department was carried out by the employees and the Industrial Health Service. The reason for this was that damping boxes irritated the operators and reduced the noise by no more than 7 dB. The "IHS" therefore made a systematic check-list for saw noise reduction.

This meant continuous trials with different saw blade r.p.m., types of blade, improved grip on the "job" and incapsulation of the saw. Control measurements showed the noise to have fallen from 95 to 81 dB(A), a reduction of 14 dB. This procedure has given the department valuable experience in noise control and the employees have gone on to work on other noise problems in the department.

Evaluation

Both the Safety Committee and the safety groups are satisfied with the work. The management has expressed satisfaction in that the noise problems have been solved and that things went well with regard to the involvement of experts. The management did not, however, think that noise assessment and practical control of noise should have been carried out by their own staff. "That's what you have experts for". The employees must have the possibility of taking position with regard to plans as well as to the assessment and possible solutions. The importance of this is underlined by the safety groups. They must be involved in the work so that things run smoothly. In the fitting department, the assessment was found to be satisfactory whilst the work with noise reduction was begun in the wrong way. The operators should have been asked for advice before standard solutions were implemented. The problems were solved in the end when they decided to do it themselves. The employees point out that the noise committee should have given more information and collaboration better.

Generally, both management and safety groups indicate that the most important thing learned from this case is that the employees must be involved, and better informed, and that machinery bought should fulfil rules and regulations.

8.4 HAZARDOUS SUBSTANCES ASSESSMENT AND CONTROL AT THE KENT CHEMICAL COMPANY LIMITED, UK.

The Kent Chemical Company specialise in the production and blending of mixtures of chemicals. They produce a large range of commercial chemical mixtures to customers specifications using over 1000 different substances. The diversity of their products requires that production is undertaken in batches. This poses specific problems for the Company in trying to ensure that substances are handled safely and with minimum risk to health for the operators. Following the introduction of the Control of Substances Hazardous to Health Regulations in 1988, a formal system for assessing and controlling risks to health and safety has been introduced.

Keywords: Company Health and Safety Policy, Thematic "Fact findind Assessment", Hazardous substances, Steering Committee, Assessment demanded by legislation.

Background

The Kent Chemical Company operate at a number a sites in the south of England but their main production facilities are situated at a site in Kent. They employ around 130 staff at the main Kent site, which is the subject of the case study. Products range from household and commercial detergents to specialist industrial cleaning products. There are also facilities for packaging of pesticides.

The main operations are the storage and issuing of substances used in blending, the batch mixing of chemicals, and the packing and dispatch of products. There are also laboratories which are used for product development and quality control. The Companies main office building is also situated at the site. There are a number of buildings and storage areas for chemicals and wastes.

The Company have always been concerned to ensure that operations are conducted safely and with minimum risk to health. However in 1988 the Control of Substances Hazardous to Health Regulations introduced a new system of legislative controls, the prime purpose of which was to ensure that Companies introduced appropriate procedures for assessing and controlling risks to health arising from the exposure to hazardous substances in the workplace. With so many different substances being used on site, and in so many different ways, it was a significant challenge for the Company to ensure that the requirements of the new Regulations were met. Therefore, they developed a sophisticated system of assessment and control which covered all aspects of materials and substances and the operations in which they were used.

Organisation of assessment for hazardous substances

The first aspect of the organisational arrangements for ensuring health and safety for workers and others likely to be affected by the Company's activities is the Company Health and Safety Policy. The Policy was developed by the Board and set out the aims of the policy, the roles and responsibilities of the Managing Director, Departmental Managers, the Safety Officer, supervisors and staff. The Policy also sets out the terms of reference for the works Safety Committee. A copy of the Policy is issued to all employees and forms part of their Contract of Employment. A summary of the main organisational structure with regards to health and safety is shown below:

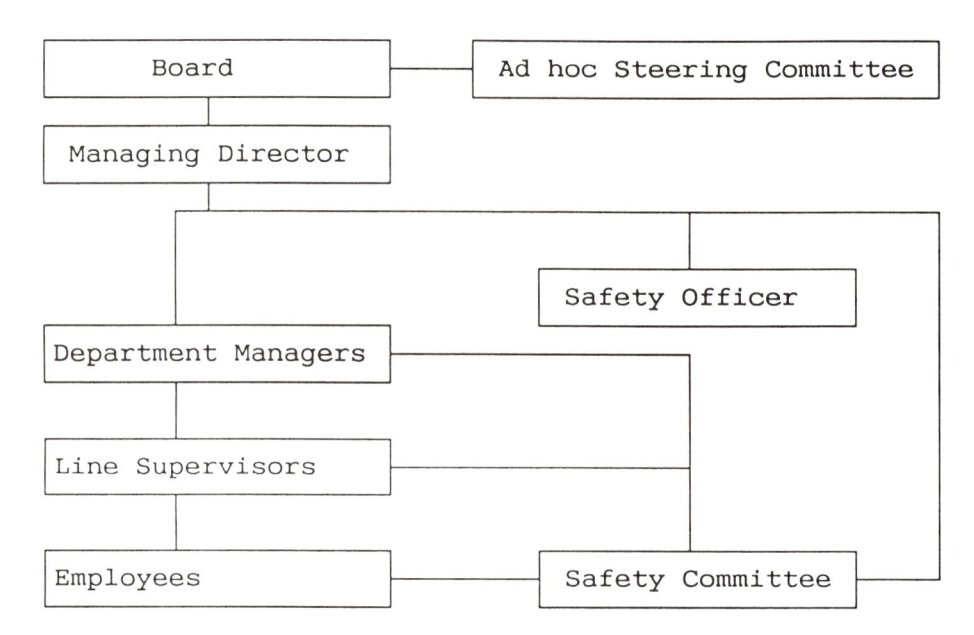

Fig. 8.4.1. **Organisational structure with regards to health and safety.**

The Health and Safety Policy also specifies general precautions and safe systems of work to be followed when handling chemicals, operating fork lift trucks, fire, electrical safety, etc. While the Health and Safety Policy gives general guidance, the nature of operations is such that the nature of hazards and risks may very considerably from batch to batch and at different stages of each operation. Therefore, the Company have developed a specific assessment procedure which is designed to allow the responsible managers within each part of the works to undertake the assessment for each operation and then to implement any controls as necessary. A full-time occupational hygienist provides specialist advice to the assessors, where appropriate, and also participates in assessments to ensure that the standard assessment procedures are followed.

Development of the works assessment procedures has been overseen by a specific Steering Committee who report to the main Board. The Steering Committee members are mainly executives and Directors of the Company. A Team Briefing system is used to inform all staff of essential health and safety matters, including the assessments of hazardous substances, and that the senior managers are made aware of problems and the views and concerns of employees. The Safety Committee made up of representatives of management and employees participate in the development of procedures and review safety matters and their communication throughout the Company. The Safety Committee also advise on employee training.

The development of the actual methods of assessment and the provision of relevant technical and scientific data is the responsibility of the Safety Officer and health and safety advisers, including the occupational hygienist. They draw upon the expert help that is available within the parent company, the Cookson Group plc.

As many of the products that are made are subject to strict confidentiality agreements, it is important that the exact ingredients of most products are not made known to employees engaged in their manufacture. However, communication of necessary safety information is essential and therefore a system of information sheets and notices has been developed to communicate such information. An example of a typical tank safety notice is given in Appendix IV, Figure 1. These are attached to all blending tanks to show what their contents are and what precautions should be followed. Line safety notices are also provided to cover the blending operations and the exact safety equipment that should be used for each batch as illustrated by Figure 8.4.2. This information is supplemented by detailed Material Safety Data Sheets which are available for inspection by employees and managers. These cover both raw materials and products as shown in Figure 8.4.3. which shows an example from raw materials and Appendix IV, Figure 2. concerning products.

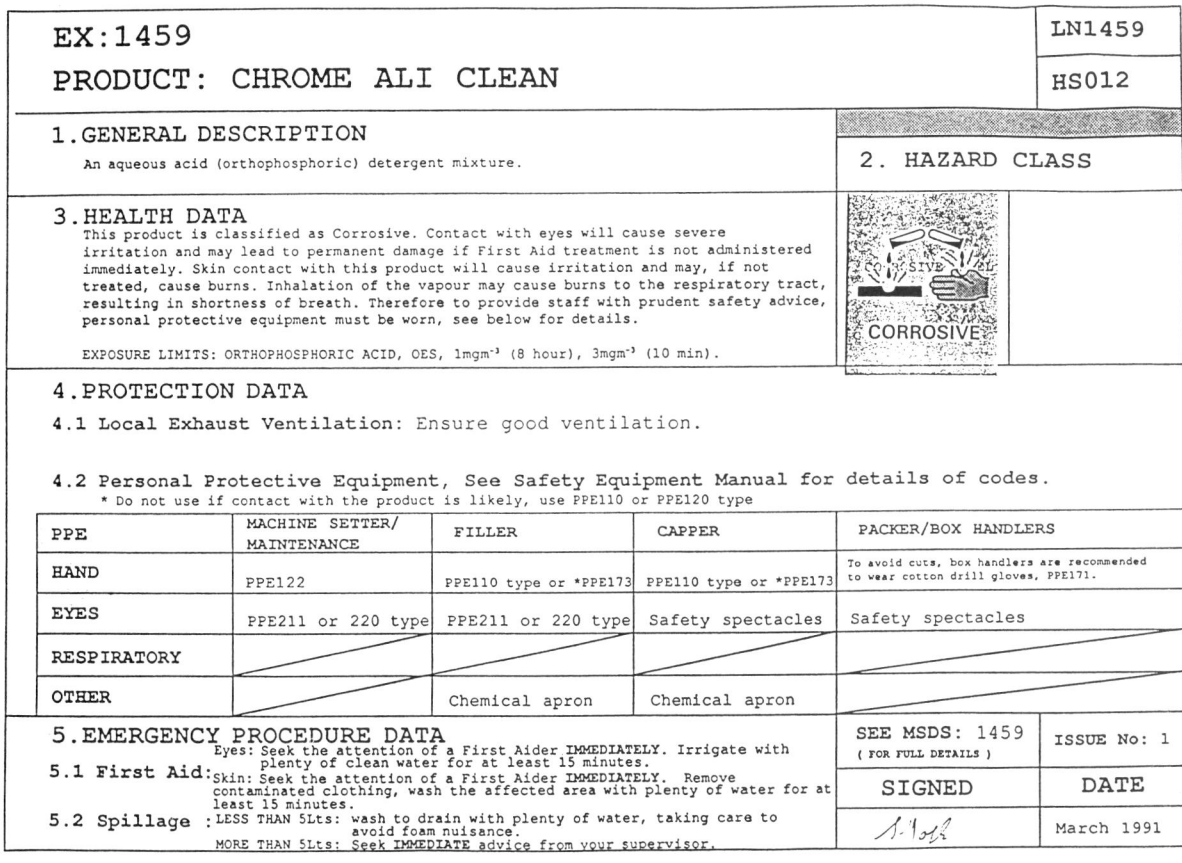

EX:1459				LN1459
PRODUCT: CHROME ALI CLEAN				HS012
1. GENERAL DESCRIPTION An aqueous acid (orthophosphoric) detergent mixture.			2. HAZARD CLASS	
3. HEALTH DATA This product is classified as Corrosive. Contact with eyes will cause severe irritation and may lead to permanent damage if First Aid treatment is not administered immediately. Skin contact with this product will cause irritation and may, if not treated, cause burns. Inhalation of the vapour may cause burns to the respiratory tract, resulting in shortness of breath. Therefore to provide staff with prudent safety advice, personal protective equipment must be worn, see below for details. EXPOSURE LIMITS: ORTHOPHOSPHORIC ACID, OES, 1mgm⁻³ (8 hour), 3mgm⁻³ (10 min).			CORROSIVE	
4. PROTECTION DATA 4.1 Local Exhaust Ventilation: Ensure good ventilation. 4.2 Personal Protective Equipment, See Safety Equipment Manual for details of codes. * Do not use if contact with the product is likely, use PPE110 or PPE120 type				

PPE	MACHINE SETTER/ MAINTENANCE	FILLER	CAPPER	PACKER/BOX HANDLERS
HAND	PPE122	PPE110 type or *PPE173	PPE110 type or *PPE173	To avoid cuts, box handlers are recommended to wear cotton drill gloves, PPE171.
EYES	PPE211 or 220 type	PPE211 or 220 type	Safety spectacles	Safety spectacles
RESPIRATORY				
OTHER		Chemical apron	Chemical apron	

5. EMERGENCY PROCEDURE DATA		
5.1 First Aid: Eyes: Seek the attention of a First Aider IMMEDIATELY. Irrigate with plenty of clean water for at least 15 minutes. Skin: Seek the attention of a First Aider IMMEDIATELY. Remove contaminated clothing, wash the affected area with plenty of water for at least 15 minutes. 5.2 Spillage : LESS THAN 5Lts: wash to drain with plenty of water, taking care to avoid foam nuisance. MORE THAN 5Lts: Seek IMMEDIATE advice from your supervisor.	SEE MSDS: 1459 (FOR FULL DETAILS)	ISSUE No: 1
	SIGNED	DATE
		March 1991

Fig. 8.4.2. Ex. of a production line safety notice showing health and safety information information and equipment required for personal protection.
(Copyright The Kent Chemical Company Ltd.)

RAW MATERIAL SAFETY DATA SHEET	CODE: L51
NAME: FORMALDEHYDE SOLUTION	HS056

1. MATERIAL DATA

1.1 Synonyms: Formalin, Methanal

1.2 CAS No: 50-00-0

1.3 Suppliers: Synthite Ltd   1.4 Container: 25Kg container

2. PHYSICAL DATA

2.1 Form: liquid   2.2 Colour: Clear water white

2.3 Odour: Pungent, irritating   2.4 Density: 1.09Kg/Ltr @ 20°C

2.5 pH: 3 - 5, neat @ 20°C   2.6 bpt °C: 96   fpt °C: 0

2.7 Sol. in water: Completely   2.8 Viscosity: <2cp @ 20°C very thin

2.9 Description: Preservative, embalming fluid

3. HEALTH HAZARDS

This material is classified as being Toxic, by inhalation, in contact with skin and if swallowed. Inhalation of the vapours will have an immediate irritation of the respiratory tract. Poisoning most commonly occurs following ingestion. Ingestion of between 100mls or less can be fatal. Contact with the eyes will cause severe burns, prolonged exposure to the vapour can cause irritation and inflammation of the eye lids. Contact with the skin will remove the natural oils causing dryness, discomfort and possibly irritation and may even lead to skin sensitisation. Therefore to provide staff with prudent safety advice, personal protective equipment must be worn when handling this material, see below for details.
OCCUPATIONAL EXPOSURE LIMITS: MEL, 2ppm (8 hour) & 2ppm (10 min)

4. PROTECTIVE MEASURES

4.1 Storage:
Store in closed, original container in a cool place under cover and away from strongly oxidising substances. Do not store with acids and in particular Hydrochloric acid and products containing these materials.

4.2 Handling:
Avoid skin contact, wear suitable gloves, overalls and apron. Take care to avoid splashing or contact with eyes, wear suitable eye protection at all times. Avoid breathing vapour, ensure adequate ventilation at all times, if available use local exhaust extraction. If inhalation is likely wear suitable respiratory protection, see below. When ever possible use siphons to decant material.

4.3 Local Exhaust Ventilation:
Use suitable extraction when available.

4.3 Personal Protective Equipment:

Hands: PPE122   Eyes: Goggles PPE211 or face shield PPE221
Respiratory: PPE11 with PPE112 or PPE115. Other: Apron
use only when below the MEL

RAW MATERIAL SAFETY DATA SHEET	CODE: L51
	HS056

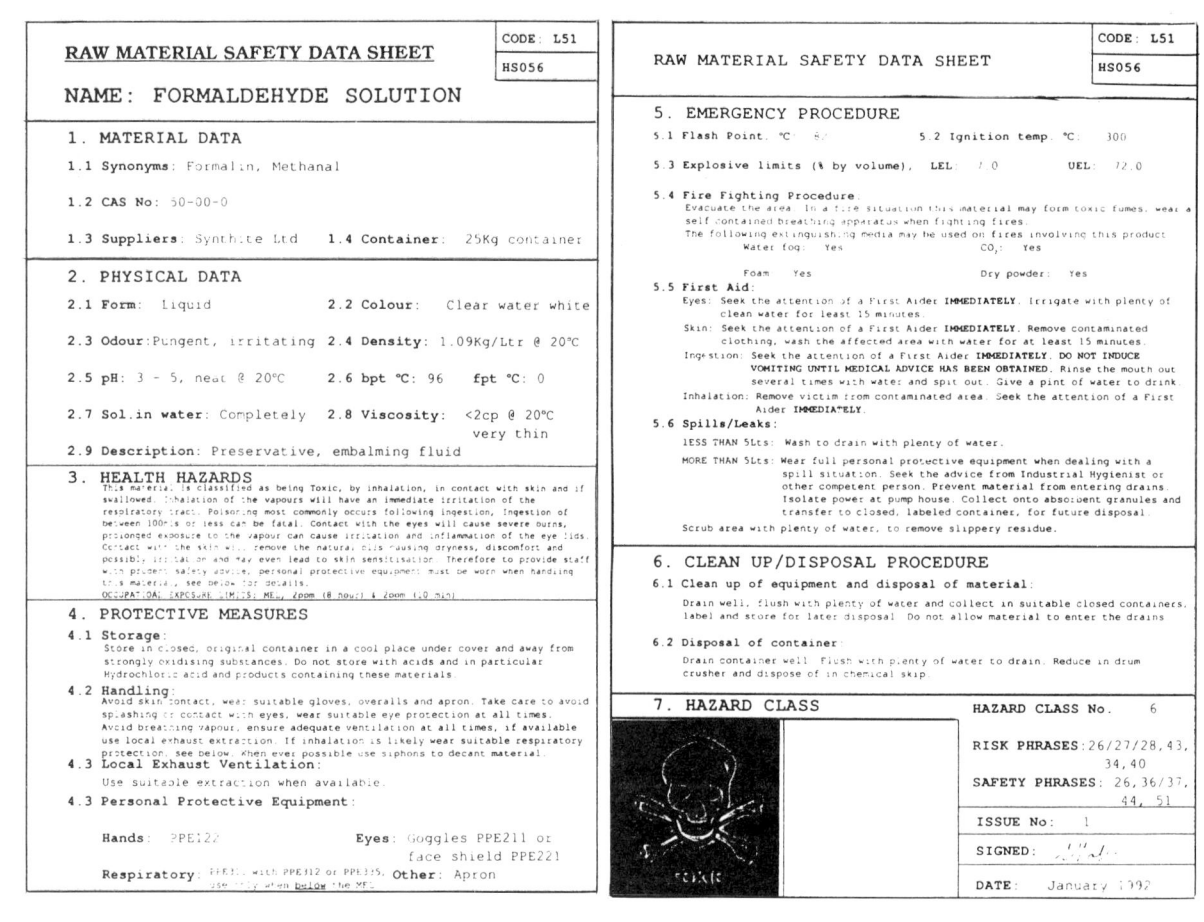

5. EMERGENCY PROCEDURE

5.1 Flash Point °C: 6?   5.2 Ignition temp. °C: 300

5.3 Explosive limits (% by volume), LEL: 7.0   UEL: 72.0

5.4 Fire Fighting Procedure:
Evacuate the area. In a fire situation this material may form toxic fumes, wear a self contained breathing apparatus when fighting fires.
The following extinguishing media may be used on fires involving this product
Water fog: Yes   CO₂: Yes
Foam: Yes   Dry powder: Yes

5.5 First Aid:
Eyes: Seek the attention of a First Aider **IMMEDIATELY**. Irrigate with plenty of clean water for least 15 minutes.
Skin: Seek the attention of a First Aider **IMMEDIATELY**. Remove contaminated clothing, wash the affected area with water for at least 15 minutes.
Ingestion: Seek the attention of a First Aider **IMMEDIATELY**. **DO NOT INDUCE VOMITING UNTIL MEDICAL ADVICE HAS BEEN OBTAINED**. Rinse the mouth out several times with water and spit out. Give a pint of water to drink.
Inhalation: Remove victim from contaminated area. Seek the attention of a First Aider **IMMEDIATELY**.

5.6 Spills/Leaks:
LESS THAN 5Lts: Wash to drain with plenty of water.
MORE THAN 5Lts: Wear full personal protective equipment when dealing with a spill situation. Seek the advice from Industrial Hygienist or other competent person. Prevent material from entering drains. Isolate power at pump house. Collect onto absorbent granules and transfer to closed, labeled container, for future disposal.
Scrub area with plenty of water, to remove slippery residue.

6. CLEAN UP/DISPOSAL PROCEDURE

6.1 Clean up of equipment and disposal of material:
Drain well, flush with plenty of water and collect in suitable closed containers, label and store for later disposal. Do not allow material to enter the drains

6.2 Disposal of container:
Drain container well, flush with plenty of water to drain. Reduce in drum crusher and dispose of in chemical skip.

7. HAZARD CLASS   HAZARD CLASS No. 6

RISK PHRASES: 26/27/28, 43, 34, 40
SAFETY PHRASES: 26, 36/37, 44, 51

ISSUE No: 1
SIGNED: ...
DATE: January 1992

Fig. 8.4.3. *Raw material safety data sheet. (Copyright The Kent Chemical Company Ltd.)*

Assessment methods

The assessment of hazards presented by subtances is conducted initially by the Safety Officer and the hygienist who collect and collate relevant technical and scientific information about hazards and measures that should be taken to minimise risk. This information is assessed to determine whether the substances or materials can be handled safely. Screening of all substances used at the site in this way has resulted in discussions to discontinue using several substances. For approved substances, Materials Safety Data Sheets are prepared to inform operators of the hazards associated with each material or product. Similar information is made available to customers for all products. Where appropriate, information is also passed on to the Poisons Unit at New Cross Hospital in the event of emergencies involving the Company products.

The assessment of hazards and risks associated with every operation conducted at the works is undertaken by the managers responsible for each area. To do this, they use a standard "Fact Findind Assessment" form which guides them through each stage of the assessment. In summary this covers the following points:

Summary of Fact Finding Assessment Checklist:

SUBSTANCES, MANUFACTURING PROCESS AND EXPOSED WORKERS	1.	Number of workers likely to be exposed.
	2.	List of all substances used including their physical state, mode of exposure and toxicity class.
	3.	Toxic effects of each substance and any relevant occupational exposure standards.
	4.	Details of the process including flow charts.
	5.	Sources of exposure.
STORAGE	6.	Storage arrangements, their adequancy and any improvements that may be required.
	7.	Whether leaks are possible and if so, how they could be prevented?
PACKAGING AND LABELLING	8.	Whether suitable packaging and labelling is provided
	9.	If not, any improvements that could be made.
TRANSPORT	10.	How are substances transported?
	11.	Whether inhalation or skin contact is possible and if so, the methods that are used to control exposure
	12.	What improvements could be made to reduce exposure further?
	13.	Are spills possible, and if so, the methods of control that would be applied?
	14.	What improvements could be made for controlling spills?
SUBSTANCE USE	15.	How the substances are used, including sketches etc?
	16.	What improvement in use could be made?
	17.	Whether inhalation or skin contact is possible, if so the methods of exposure control that are used?
	18.	What improvements could be made to reduce exposure further?
DISPOSAL	19.	How is disposal of wastes or surplus substances achieved?
	20.	Is inhalation or skin contact possible, and if so what are the methods of control?
	21.	What improvements could be made?
INTERMEDIATE PRODUCTS	22.	Whether any intermediates may be produced and whether these could be emitted into the work area?
	23.	Is inhalation or skin contact possible, and if so how would it be controlled.
WORKPLACE MONITORING	24.	Whether airborne concentrations are measured, and if so their frequency, results, etc.
	25.	If not, should measurements be made.
	26.	Do the results show that a hazard to health exists?
	27.	Are surface contamination measurements necessary?
HEALTH/MEDICAL SURVEILLANCE	28.	Details of any health/medical surveillance that is required or undertaken.
BIOLOGICAL MONITORING	29.	Are biological measurements taken and if so, their frequency, results, etc?
	30.	Do the results of any biological monitoring show risks to health?

VENTILATION METHODS OF CONTROL	31. 32.	If ventilation methods of control are used, their frequency, routine measurement results etc. Do results show any malfunctioning of the systems.
PROTECTIVE EQUIPMENT	33. 34. 35. 36.	The type, selection, inspection and maintenance arrangements for protective equipment. Is the protective equipment suitable and in good working order? Are any improvements required? Is decontamination of protective equipment necessary, and if so, when and how is it undertaken?
OTHER METHODS OF CONTROL	37. 38.	Are any other methods of control used, and are they working satisfactorily? If not, what improvements could be made?
TRAINING	39. 40.	Do the work methods require any special training? Is training adequate to minimise risks to health and if not what extra training is required?
WELFARE AND PERSONAL HYGIENE	41. 42.	What provisions are made and are they satisfactory? If not, what improvements could be made?
HEALTH AND SAFETY WORK SHEETS	43. 44.	Are any health and safety work sheets issued? If not, should they be issued and what should appear on such sheets?
EMISSIONS TO ATMOSPHERE	45. 46.	What emissions to atmosphere are likely to occur? Are they likely to cause any environmental problems, and if so how can these be minimised?
THE ASSESSMENT CONCLUSION	47. 48.	In the opinion of the assessor, taking into account the toxic nature of the substances and the way in which they were observed to be used and controlled, does a risk to health occur? If yes, how, where and what improvements are required to minimise the hazards or to achieve satisfactory control?
THE ASSESSOR	49. 50.	Details of their name, position and qualifications. Their signature and date.
REASSESSMENT	51.	Whether work conditions are likely to change substantially in the foreseeable future, and if so when should a reassessment be conducted?

Once these assessments have been carried out, the data is correlated and analysed and then reviewed by the Steering Committee who considers whether or not action is required, and if so what action is appropriate. This is then reviewed by the Steering Committee who make appropriate recommendations to the Board or specific managers as appropriate.

Assessments are conducted for all areas of the works and for all operations, including production, maintenance, offices, laboratories, transport and storage. Where appropriate, workers are observed throughout the operations to see what they actually do, and they may be questioned about their views and experiences. The general findings and conclusions are received and acknowledged to the Safety Committee for their consideration.

Evaluation

The structured approach that has been developed by The Kent Chemical Company for the identification and assessment of problems and possible solutions allows the Company to determine where the main issues lie and what actions could be taken to alleviate specific difficulties.

By placing the responsibility for assessment in the hands of the managers responsible for each area, the works ensures that the assessments are representative and that the managers who make to day-to-day decisions are fully aware of the implications of such decisions. This also ensures that expert advice and assistance is only sought where necessary and is targeted to those areas where it is likely to give greatest benefit.

The main problem that still remains to be resolved is finding ways in which the employees can be more actively involved in the identification and resolution of problems. The confidentiality constraints which govern many of the issues under consideration pose a major problem for the Company. A further problem, and one which faces almost all companies, is the limited resources that can be drawn on to implement solutions to problems. The costs of providing controls where operations are intermittent or only rarely undertaken may be prohibitive. However, by seeking out problems and attempting to set priorities, at least Kent Chemicals can ensure that resources that are available are targeted to areas which will give greatest return.

8.5. ENCOURAGING EMPLOYEE PARTICIPATION IN WORKPLACE AND ENVIRONMENTAL ASSESSMENT AT HOLDEN HYDROMAN PLC, UK.

Holden Hydroman plc is a leading manufacturer of painted plastics for the automotive industry. They are based in the small town of Bromyard in the County of Hereford and Worcester, England. As the major employer in the town, the Company have been striving to encourage greater employee job satisfaction and to foster active participation in improving Company performance across a wide range of business activities. As part of their efforts to develop worker participation in improving workplace and general environmental conditions around the works, Holden Hydroman have developed new systems of work organisation that allow employees to take an active role in identifying and assessing problems.

Keywords: Change of work organisation, employees participation, management of change, Personal Action Plans.

Background

The Company employs over a hundred staff at their site in Bromyard, Hereford and Worcestershire. The main products are painted body components for the automotive industry. The Company has expanded significantly over the last ten years and is now the leading employer in the town.

The site includes offices, painting and moulding facilities, and general materials storage areas. A large new paint plant has recently been built to allow for expansion and to relieve heavy pressure on the existing spray paint facilities. The manufacturing and finishing of products involves using a variety of machinery and solvent based paints. Given the inherent hazards associated with the substances being used and the nature of the manufacturing operations, the Company have developed extensive safety management policies and procedures. In addition, the advanced specifications for their products has meant that sophisticated systems of quality assurance have also been introduced.

With the continual need to make the business more efficient and effective, the management identified that there were a number of key problems facing the Company. In summary, these were that costs were too high, productivity was too low, customers were given comparative poor service and there was too many rejects and customer returns. With this as a background, they sought to identify the various causes of the problems that they were experiencing. The quality of the working environment, safety and housekeeping and the inadequacies of communication and participation within the workforce were all identified among the possible causes. The managers therefore initiated a programme of measures to omprove the performance of the Company by tackling some of these fundamental causes.

The measures that were introduced included the development of better systems for identifying and assessing problems, and in particular for encouraging workers to take on some of the responsibility for improving working conditions.

The basic aims were explained to all managers and workers through the Company Mission Statement which set the following aims:

- to provide products and service which delights customers.
- to work together and with customers and suppliers, in harmony, and with the same aims and in a manner based on logic, respect, honesty and mutual trust.
- to work continously towards the identification and elimination of waste throughout all aspects of the business.
- to operate a safe and pleasant working environment.

Gaining employee involvement

In setting the aims outlined above, it was recognised from the start that the process of gaining active participation of workers would be difficult given the considerable organisational inertia that was evident. However, a Steering Committee at executive level was formed to oversee the development of various initiatives. The Steering Committee is made up of Directors and senior managers of the Company. One of these was to involve all employees in identifying and resolving problems specific to their own areas of operation and in so doing to let workers believe that their input was seen to be important and valued. Workers were encouraged to form groups, each of which was given the aim of improving the quality of their own working environment. Each group was allocated a leader who was made responsible for liaison with the management.

The groups are supported by a Facilitator whose role is to help them develop and express their ideas and to identify and make available the resources and expertise to allow the development of these ideas.

Assessments

The Company have developed a clear and succinct system of responsibilities for identifying and resolving workplace and environmental problems. This operates at two levels: firstly in terms of day-to-day problems; and secondly during the planning and design og new projects, facilities, plant and in the purchasing of equipment, supplies etc.

The organisation arrangements for identifying problems occurring during routine operations and for maintaining safe and healthy working conditions is as follows:

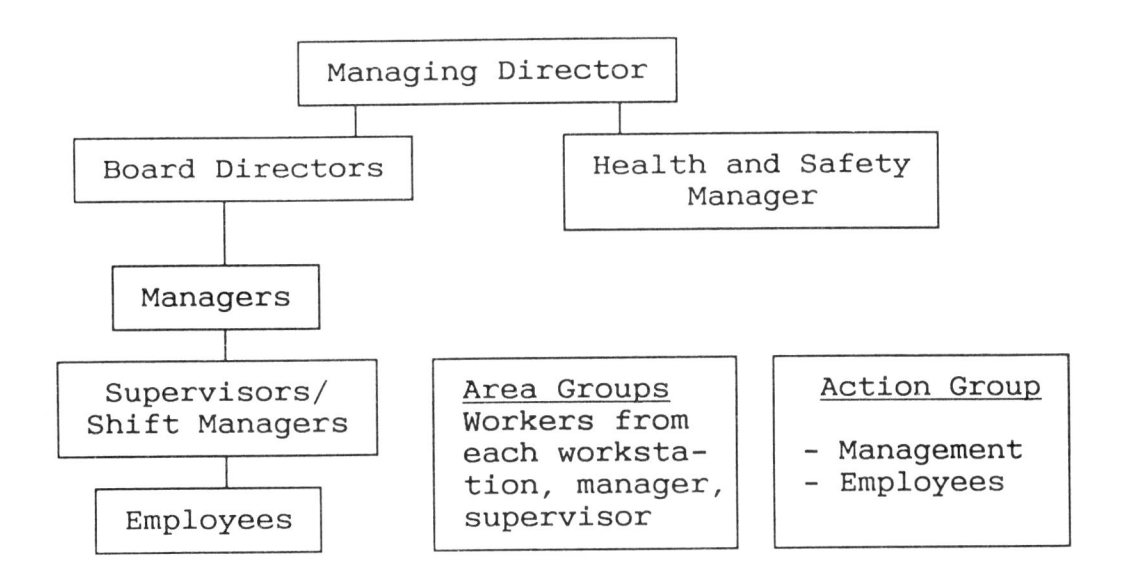

Fig. 8.5.1. Organisational structure with regards to health and safety.

Specific responsibilities for ensuring that health, safety and environmental issues are taken into account in all new developments are allocated as:

- Operations Director - in the planning stages of major changes in Company operations.
- Sales and Marketing Director - in the planning stage of new projects.
- Executive Manager, Technical Centre - in the assessment of the impact of new projects.

With the help of the Facilitator, each group develops Personal Action Plans which summarise the nature of the problem or concern and then helps guide the team through the process of identifying the cause and ways in which this can be measured. The Plans then highlight the people who need to be involved in assessing the problem and identifying long term solutions. An example is given in Figure 8.5.2. Overall control of the decisions about what priorities are given to assessing and resolving problems is the responsibility of the manager in charge of each area of the works.

PERSONAL ACTION PLAN				NAME:	Manager,	
				DEPARTMENT	Area A	
NO.	CONCERN	BASIC CAUSE	METHOD OF MEASUREMENT	TEAM	LONGTERM SOLUTION	WHEN
(4) EQUIP	CLEANING OF PLANT IS INADEQUATE	LACK OF PROCEDURE/ SUPERVISION AND LACK OF FIRST HAND KNOWLEDGE OF THE PLANT	F.T.R./POLISHING EXTRACTION READINGS, BREAKDOWN RECORDINGS MAINTENANCE CLEANING COST TO STANDARD	S GROGAN S HALLING S HILL A HARPER PP PRICE R MEREDITH T KIRKHAM	LAID DOWN CLEANING PROCEDURES WITH CORRECT LEVEL OF SUPERVISION ON AN AGREED REGULARITY OF CLEANING I.E. ONCE A WEEK/2 WEEKS/MONTH	
(3) PEOPLE	CONTROL ON MATERIAL HANDLING	NO LAID DOWN SET PROCEDURES OR SYSTEMS. INEFFICENT SHOP FLOOR LAYOUT	THE SYSTEM REDUCTION OF OPERATOR MOVEMENT	J HUCKLE A CUFFLEY D MATTHEWS K POWELL L BURNHAM J ILIFF		

Fig. 8.5.2. *Example of Personal Action Plan (Copyright: Holden Hydroman Ltd.).*

While the nature of the problems addressed by each group may vary, some problems are best tackled at a more general level. These are dealt with by an Action Group which holds regular meetings at which any matter of concern can be raised. The Action Group has three manager representatives with the remaining posts being taken up by worker representatives from each area of the works. As there is no formal safety committee, the Action Group also acts in this capacity.

Most assessments are handled internally, although external consultants are occasionally brought in to advise on technical matters such as noise monitoring and control and the assessment of risks associated with hazardous substances. The works Health and Safety Manager is generally responsible for briefing and liaison with external advisers. The Company Medical Officer deals with health and medical surveillance problems. Similarly, external environmental problems tend to be dealt with by consultants and the local environmental health department. For example, following complaints of odour in the local neighbourhood, the local authority collaborated with the Company in a joint exercise to monitor emissions from the paint spray plant and to assess whether any additional controls should be applied.

Evaluation

Whilst the methods of encouraging employee participation in workplace and environmental assessment at Holden Hydroman are a comparative recent innovation, the Company is convinced that this will help to improve employee job fatisfaction and commitment whilst also ensuring that a better quality working environment is achieved. The changes that have been introduced are still new and have yet to be fully appreciated by much of the workforce, but the systems that have been put in place go a long way to meeting many of the problems that the Company have experienced.

Appendix I

References

1. WHO basic documents - 38th edition (1990) Geneva, p. 1.

2. EC, The economically and social committee, Report from the department for social affairs, file No. SOC/33, doc. KOM (77) 657 endel, Brussels the 13. of June 1978.

3. Jensen, P.L. and Drachmann, J., 1989, Guidelines to workplace assessment, The Work Environment Fund, DK

4. Cronberg, T. et al., 1981, Planning of buildings: Briefing. Pupl. No. 131, Danish Building Research Institute, DK

5. Flagstad, S.M. and Laustsen, S., 1984, Methods of planning industrial work environment, The Work Environment Fund, DK

6. Clausen, C. and Lorentzen, B. 1986, Participation in implementation of new technology, Danish Technological Institute, Human Ressources Development.

7. Kirkegaard, O. & Prag, S., 1983, Participation in the planning of work environment - by alterations and enlargements of the company, The Work Environment Fund, DK

8. Møller, N. et al., 1988, Action methods of the Safety Group, The Work Environment Fund, DK

9. Confederation of British Industry (1990), Narrowing the Gap, Environmental Auditing Guidelines for Business, Confederation of British Industry, London.

10. United Nations Programme, Environmental Auditing, UNEP Report No. 2.

11. International Chamber of Commerce (1990), Environmental Auditing, International Chamber of Commerce, London.

12. International Chamber of Commerce (1988), Environmental Auditing, ICC Position Paper on Environmental Auditing, London.

13. Thomas, M.S. (1991), Safety Auditing, The Safety and Health Practitioner, December, pp. 28-30.

14. Health And Safety Technology And Management Ltd. (1991), Environment Audit: A complete guide to undertaking an environmental audit for your business, Merarry Business Books, Northants.

15. Bamber, L. (1990), Risk Management: techniques and practices. In Safety at work, Editor Ridley J.R. Butterworth - Heinemann Ltd., ISBN 0-7506-1018.

16. Chemical Industries Association Ltd., *A Guide to Hazard and Operability Studies*, Chemical Industries Association, London (1977).

17. Kiil, O. & Heide, J., 1986, *Work environment and technical planning*, The Work Environment Fund, DK

18. *Hazards from organic solvents, Health and Safety experiences and technical measures*, The Swedish Work Environment Fund, 1982

19. Schneider, T. et al., 1986, *Technical Occupational Hygiene*, Danish National Institute of Occupational Health, DK

20. Jensen, P.L. & Stranddorf, J., 1991, *Survey of the work environment of the company*, The Danish Technical University, Department of Work Environment.

21. European Council Directive 89/391/EEC *on the introduction of measures to encourage improvements in the safety and health of workers at work*.

22. European Council Directive 85/337/EEC *on the assessment of the effects of certain public and private projects on the environment*.

Appendix II

Industrial Hygiene Assessment Manual

The Industrial Hygiene Assessment Manual comprises (this introduction) a list of questions, and a summary sheet: The Safety Report. It is a tool, for use by small and medium sized companies and factories, in connection with <u>industrial hygiene</u>, <u>the general outdoor environment</u> and <u>safety at work</u> and can be used for systematic identification of problems, a regular safety check and in management decision making with regard to health and safety work. Such essential decisions relate to the company's work environment and general environment policies, conditions for health and safety work and allocation of assignments and responsibility for the work. The questions in the Industrial Hygiene Survey are divided up under the following sub-headings:

A. Company policy, management, and cooperation agreements.

B. The interior design and technical installations of the workplace.

C. Machine and tool safety.

D. Hazardous chemicals and materials.

E. Air quality.

F. Noise and vibration.

G. Physiological factors.

H. Organistion of work and psychological factors.

I. Lighting.

J. Thermal factors.

The manual embraces the topics which are found to be the most important and useful at company level. Questions concerning i.e. biological factors must be added if needed.

WHAT CAN THE MANUAL BE USED FOR?

The manual is built up of series of questions. Questions on: identifying the problem, identifying the cause, the need for professional help in investigating a problem and finding a solution, taking steps, responsibility for seeing that the steps are carried out, and instructing the employees.

By putting these questions, the manual not only focuses on the identification of problems, but also systematically records health and safety arrangements which are already in use and in good working order. The manual therefore also presents a systematic and meaningful way of tackling health and safety work.

WHO CAN USE THE MANUAL?

The manual can be used on different levels and by different interested parties. For example, over the whole company and by the company's health and safety group, or by a single representative in connection with a single workstation. The questions ought to be gone through and filled out with both a person in a position of authority and an employee representative since the answers and the settlement of problems require experience with management, production, work environment and environmental considerations.

HOW TO USE THE MANUAL

The company's work environment and environmental condition should be able to be checked without unnecessary amounts of administration and forms to be filled out. Therefore, decisions reached are listed on a report form: <u>Company Safety Report</u>. The decisions must be attended to, not just registered. By this it is assumed that the important thing to do at company level is to make decisions. If also the registered problems needs attendance, an alternative summary sheet must be prepared.

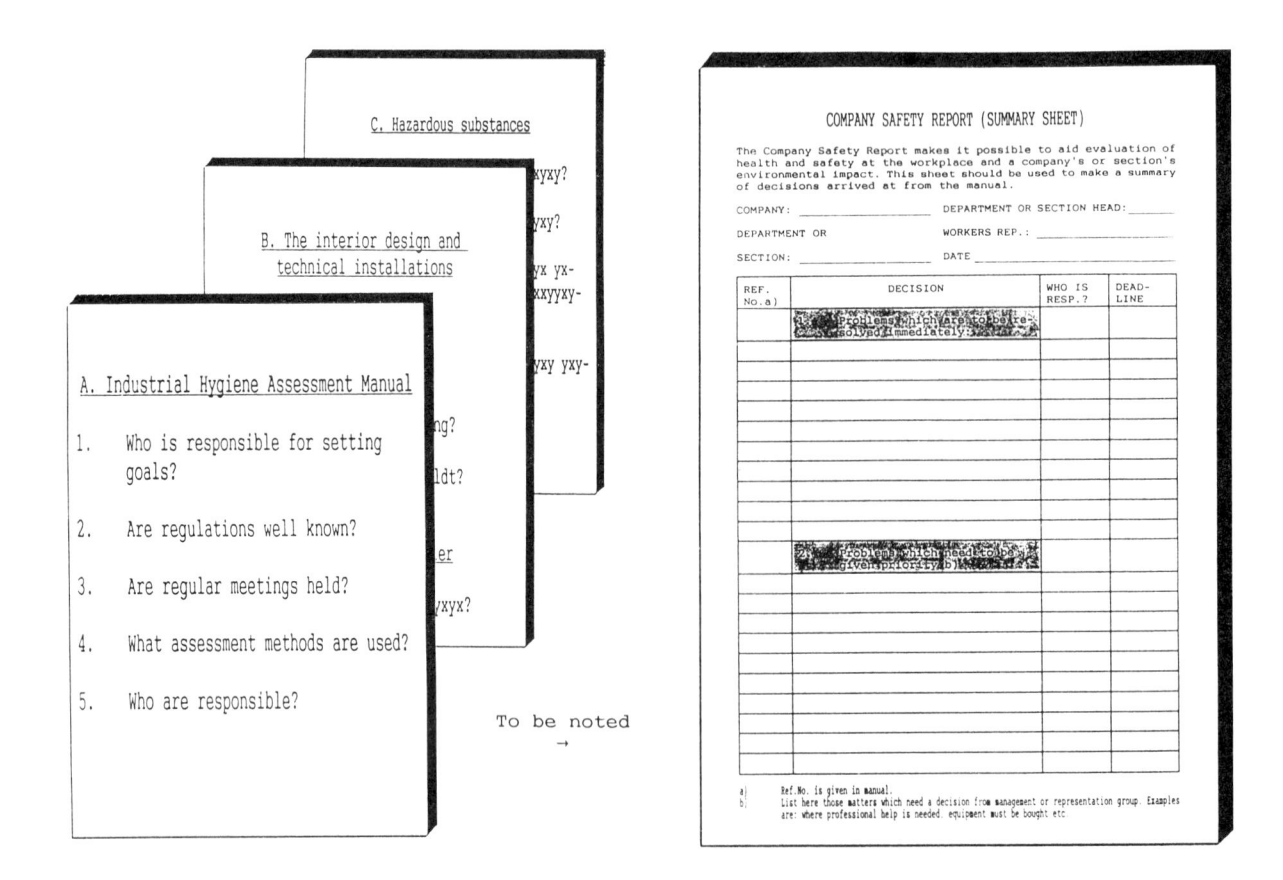

Fig. 1. Using the check list system.

The survey must ensure both that small and easily solved problems are resolved immediately and, at the same time, that problems which will have to be discussed by the management, or by meetings of concerned parties, are registered. Therefore, the Report sheet is divided up into two parts:

1. Problems which are to be resolved immediately.
2. Problems which need to be given priority.

Typical examples of Problems which might be listed under point 2 are: starting up a professional investigation, implementation of expensive equipment, evaluating new work methods and organisation and starting up employee involvement schemes. The company's health and safety group's job is to prioritise work and get things moving. See Fig. 2. (20)

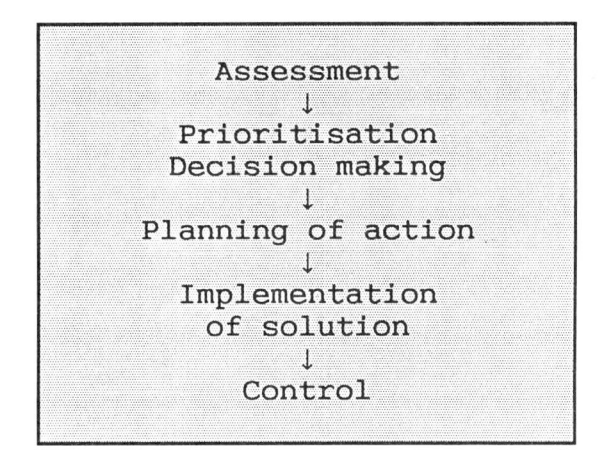

```
Assessment
    ↓
Prioritisation
Decision making
    ↓
Planning of action
    ↓
Implementation
of solution
    ↓
Control
```

Fig. 2. Assessment procedure

GETTING STARTED

One risk with checklists is that they are not used. Two of the main reasons for this are: that they are seldom aimed directly at the situation they are used for; and that the survey is not given full backing by the management.

It is essential then, that the survey is supported from the start: by ensuring that enough time is set aside, and possibly also by fine-tuning the questions so that their relevance to the work being carried out can be more easily seen. Introductory seminars with involvement of external consultants can be one way of ensuring more successful surveys.

It is also essential to ensure the support of the management and to ensure that participation in the survey is obligatory for all concerned. Clarification of the company policies concerning work environment, environment, safety at work and not to say the cooperation agreements are then important issues.

Industrial Hygiene Assessment Manual

For use in assessing a company's or section's workplace environment and the company's influence on the general outdoor environment.

A. Company policy, management and cooperation agreements

Setting of goals (standards) and means for carrying them out

A.1. Who is responsible for setting goals (standards) with regard to Safety, Health, outdoor environment, control and inspection, purchasing, maintenance, education and information?

A.2. Are the goals and standards approved of and supported by both the management and the employees?

A.3. Who keeps a check on the progression towards goals?

A.4. Who is responsible for seeing that regulations are known with regard to environmental health and safety?

A.5. Who is responsible for working out the budget for environmentally related work eg. investigations, aquisitions, maintenance and education?

Health and safety and areas of responsibility

A.6. Are regular meetings held?

A.7. Is the opinion of the workers taken into account with regard to health and safety work?

A.8. Who is responsible for writing minutes, define tasks, and for drawing up a list of responsibility together with deadlines?

A.9. Is time set aside for improvement of meetings?

A.10 How are employees informed on work done in connection with industrial hygiene?

A.11. What systematic methods are used for the registration of problems?

A.12. Who is responsible for registering and reporting on accidents and injuries?

A.13. Is special attention paid to particular groups (eg. pregnant women) in the course of health and safety work?

A.14. Are the management and staff well enough educated?

A.15. Who is responsible for ensuring that the work- and general environment are taken into account in the purchasing of goods and equipment?

A.16. Who is responsible for ensuring that work- and general environment are considered during the planning of new production and changes in existing production?

A.17. Is the opinion of the employees concerned considered during the planning of new production and changes in existing production?

B. The interior design and technical installations of the workplace

The interior design of the workplace

B.1. Are the law's requirements fulfilled with regard to working and eating areas, wardrobes, changing rooms, washing facilities and toilets?

B.2. Is there sufficient space?

B.3. Who is responsible for maintenance of buildings, premises, offices etc.?

B.4. Who is responsible for cleaning and tidying work areas, equipment, work stations and machines?

B.5. Who is responsible for cleaning and tidying eating areas, wardrobes, changing rooms, wahing facilities and toilets?

B.6. Is the law satisfied with respect to emergency exits?

B.7. Is there risk of falling because of slippery or uneven floors?

B.8. Does internal transport take place safely and without delays?

Technical installations

B.9. Are work areas and individual work stations sufficiently well lit?

B.10. Is there sufficient heating and ventilation?

B.11. Are there problems which are due to other technical installations, for example the electricity supply?

B.12. Who is responsible for maintenance and cleaning of lightning?

B.13. Who is responsible for instructing employees with regard to correct service of heating and ventilation devices, for example, thermostats, dampers, fans?

B.14. Who is responsible for the service and maintenance of the heating and ventilation systems?

B.15. Is there a service contract on the heating and ventilation system?

B.16. Has a report been written on the function, setting-up, running and maintenance of the ventilation system?

C. Safety in the use of tools and machinery

C.1. Who is responsible for safety in the department?

C.2. Do the machines, machine assessories, aids, transport equipment and tools fulfil the law's safety requirements?

C.3. Is there any danger that of an accident (eg. trapping, cutting, pressure-rise) being caused by carrying out work or setting up machinery?

C.4. Can the reason for accident-risk be identified?

C.5. Could an accident result in consequences for **the outdoor environment**?

C.6. Have measures been established for combatting the hazard? For example, are hazardous areas isolated from the surroundings and has any special safety equipment been installed?

C.7. Who controls and maintains safety equipment?

C.8. Who is responsible for personal protection equipment: purchase, maintenance, control of use?

C.9. Who is responsible for informing employees about accident risk, is there an instruction manual available?

C.10. Who is responsible for instructing employees in how the work should be carried out?

D. Safety when using chemicals and hazardous materials

D.1. Who is responsible for chemicals and materials in connection with work, the general outdoor environment and with fire and explosion risk?

D.2. Is the law satisfied with regard to use of chemicals and hazardous materials?

D.3. Who is responsible for listing hazardous chemicals and materials?

D.4. Are the least hazardous chemicals and materials used in each case?

The work environment

D.5. Is there a risk of damage to health through for example, contact with eyes and/or skin, inhalation, consumption?

D.6. Can the use of the chemicals and materials lead to irritation?

D.7. Is the reason for those health effects identified?

D.8. Is there a need for professional evaluation of the problem?

D.9. Have measures been taken which effectively combat the dangers, for example encapsulation and point source removal?

D.10. Who is responsible for rutine control and maintenance of the ventilation equipment etc.

D.11. Who is responsible for personal protection equipment: purchase, maintenance and control of use?

D.12. Who is responsible for making sure that hazardous chemicals and materials are kept in the ways required by law and supplier?

D.13. Who is responsible for instruction and other safety information?

D.14. Who is responsible for instructing the employees on how work should be carried out?

Outdoor environment: air pollution, waste water, solid waste, ground pollution, accidents

D.15. Is there risk of environmental damage due to chimney gases, waste water, solid waste, ground pollution or via an accident?

D.16. Can the reason for environmental damage be identified?

D.17. Is there a need or requirement for control with professional evaluation of environmental impact?

D.18. Have effective measures been established for combatting the risk of environmental damage?

D.19. Who is responsible for ensuring that the effectiveness of these measures is maintained?

D.20. Who is responsible for instructing the employees on safety procedures in the area?

Fire and explosion risk

D.21. Are flammable or explosive substances used?

D.22. Is there need or requirement for professional evaluation of fire or explosion risk?

D.23. Have effective control measures been established, for example, fire fighting equipment?

D.24. Who is responsible for ensuring that the effectiveness of these measures and equipment is maintain?

D.25. Who is responsible for instructing the employees of safety proceedures in the area?

E. Air quality

E.1. Is air quality a problem in the **work environment** or in the **general outdoor environment**? Examples: smoke, dust, smells, steam, gases, many people in the same room.

E.2. Are people annoyed by poor air quality? Example, is there a problem with irritated respiratory passages, dry air, exposure to steam, lack of fresh air?

E.3. Is it possible to describe or identify the reason for the poor quality of the air?

E.4. Is there a need or requirement for professional help in connection with this problem?

E.5. Is monitoring of the air quality required?

E.6. Have effective measures been established? Examples: encapsulation, point source removal, filtering, general ventilation.

E.7. Who is responsible for the rutine checking and maintenance of these measures?

E.8. Who is responsible for personal protection equipment? Is it maintained? Is it used?

E.9. Who is responsible for instructing employees on work methods?

F. Noise and vibration

F.1. Is noise/vibration a problem in **the work environment** or **the general outdoor environment**?

F.2. Are people annoyed by noise/vibration? Are there complaints?

F.3. Is there need for professional help with regard to this problem?

F.4. Is there a requirement for surveyance or monitoring?

F.5. Can the source of noise and/or vibration be described and identified?

F.6. Is the least noisy/vibrating method applied?

F.7. Is the noise source encapsulated/insulated?

F.8. Is the working area acoustically regulated?

F.9. Who is responsible for the maintenance of machines and tools?

F.10. Who is responsible for the maintenance of noise reduction devices?

F.11. Who is responsible for pesonal safety equipment? Is it maintained? Is it used?

G. Physiological factors

G.1. Are there any known health effects resulting from physical aspects of the work? Examples: illnesses, pains, neck pains, lumbago, pains in the shoulders, or arms?

G.2. Is there annoyance or complaint connected to the physical aspects of the work? Examples: tiredness, tenderness, pains, headaches?

G.3. Is the source of the problem known? Can it be described and identified?

G.4. Are there particular positions (eg. bending) which are found stressful?

G.5. Are there long periods of sitting, walking, or standing work?

G.6. Must heavy objects be lifted?

G.7. Do periods of monotonous work occur?

G.8. Is there need for professional help with the problem?

G.9. Is the workplace sensibly designed/laid-out? Examples: space between work stations, heights of surfaces, distances of things which must be reached.

G.10. Are appropriate working capacity (man power), machines, and tools allocated?

G.11. Are the required work aids available eg. for lifting, level adjustment and internal transport?

G.12. Who is responsible for the care and maintenance of these work aids?

H. Organisation of work and psychological factors

H.1. Is the organisation of work or other psycological aspects of the work environment considered a problem?

H.2. Does the work offer challenges to the employee or is it considered monotonous?

H.3. Is the work to demanding, for example, does it cause tiredness and over extertion?

H.4. Is the work stressful? Is the tempo too high? Is the tempo set by the machinery or by time pressures (deadlines)? Do people have to work alone?

H.5. Can the reason for psychological work environment problems be described and identified?

H.6. Is there a need for a professional help in investigating/solving the problem?

H.7. Have any industrial relations aggreement been made which aim to improve the situation? For example, has work allocation, required qualifications, the break system and/or employee education and training been improved?

H.8. Is the work organised so that cooperation and social contact is made possible?

H.9. Is the work organised such that each employee has a say in how his or her work is best carried out?

H.10 Are the employees encouraged to express their views with regard to changes in organisation?

I. Lighting

I.1. Is there access to daylaight and can people look outside through windows?

I.2. Is there sufficient general lighting?

I.3. Is the lighting of each workstation acceptable?

I.4. Is there complaint or annoyance due to lighting eg. glare, flicker, poor contrast, reflections?

I.5. Can the source of the problem be described and identified?

I.6. Is there need for professional advice?

I.7. Have measures been taken to help ease the problem eg. workstation lighting, glare-free fittings, choise of surface colour?

I.8. Who is responsible for checking and maintenance of lighting?

J. Thermal factors

J.1. Do temperatures apropriately match the type of work which is to be carried out?

J.2. Is there annoyance due, for example, to draft, too high or too low temperature, too large temperature swings, cold feet or high humidity?

J.3. Can the sources of annoyance be identified and described, for example, heat sources, gaps, site of building, sunlight?

J.4. Is there need for professional advice?

J.5 Have effective measures been taken eg. lay-out, design, furnishing of the buildings interior, insulation, suitable working clothes?

J.6. Who is responsible for maintenance and service of the heating and ventilation?

J.7. Who is responsible for employee information or instruction with regard to heating and ventilation?

COMPANY SAFETY REPORT (SUMMARY SHEET)

The Company Safety Report makes it possible to aid evaluation of health and safety at the workplace and a company's or section's environmental impact. This sheet should be used to make a summary of decisions arrived at from the manual.

COMPANY: _____   DEPARTMENT OR SECTION HEAD: _____

DEPARTMENT OR   WORKERS REP.: _____

SECTION: _____   DATE _____

REF. No.a)	DECISION	WHO IS RESP.?	DEAD-LINE
	1. Problems which are to be resolved immediately:		
	2. Problems which need to be given priority b)		

a) Ref.No. is given in manual.
b) List here those matters which need a decision from management or representation group. Examples are: where professional help is needed, equipment must be bought etc.

Appendix III

Assessment techniques.

As has been shown in Section 6 of the main body of the report, there are a wide range of different workplace and environmental assessment methods that can be applied by both companies and their expert advisers. While many of the individual methods may be highly complex, most follow a straightforward and easily understood structure. In this appendix, we have analysed a selected range of assessments that are routinely used to identify and resolve workplace or environmental problems. The purpose of the analysis has been to show that all follow a simple and logical structure that can be easily understood by anyone involved in organising or conducting assessments.

In the following examples, we have broken down each assessment into six key stages and then give a brief explanation of what may be involved at each stage. These six stages are as follows:

1. Problem identification. Examples of the information that may lead a company or an assessor to the conclusion that a problem exists. This box represents the motivation for undertaking the particular assessment.

2. Criteria. This box includes examples of the criteria that may be used in each particular example. Criteria are those key markers against which the significance of information on a problem can be evaluated.

3. Information. Examples of the information that may be gathered as the basis of each assessment.

4. Evaluation. Examples of the methods and other techniques that may be used in evaluating the significance of the problem.

5. Solutions. This box gives examples of the types of solutions that may be used to control problems that may be judged to warrant action.

6. Participants. Examples of the groups who may be involved at the Company level, as experts or assessors.

In the following the No. of the boxes refers to these 6 stages.

TYPE OF ASSESSMENT: Health and Safety Audit - Proactive system to provide managers with indicators that the risks within the organisation are being effectively controlled and that the Health and Safety Policy is achieving it's objectives.

1. Sampling specific predetermined aspects of health and safety in order to test reliability and accuracy of the Health and Safety Management System.

    Audits organised around check-lists of all issues relevant to an activity or operation.

    Audits specifically designed to investigate specific aspects of an activity or operation, eg risk management, fire safety etc.

    Identification of major hazards arising from activities and potential means of reducing risk.

2. * Company policy, procedures and systems.
   * Legal requirements
   * Other requirements: insurance

3. Interviews: management, employees representatives, enforcing agencies.
   * Sampling.
   * Physical measurements.
   * Observations.
   * Records.
   * Accidents/sickness records.

4. * Audit systems:
        ISRS
        BSC Five Star
        DuPont
        CHASE
        COURSAFE.
   * In-house scoring systems, check-lists, etc.
   * Outputs aim to disclose strengths and weaknesses and main areas of vulnerability and risk. Ranking of issues requiring detailed investigation/attention and recommended action lists.

5. * Policy changes.
   * Enforcement of policy.
   * Changes in procedures.
   * Changes in responsibilities.
   * Changes in systems of management.
   * Training.
   * Communications.
   * Detailed assessments of risks identified. Etc.

6. * Audit teams including:
        Managers
        Health and Safety Advisers
        Specialists.

TYPE OF ASSESSMENT: Environmental Audit - Proactive system to provide managers with indicators that the risks within the organisation are being effectively controlled and that the Environmental Policy is achieving it's objectives. Environmental Audits may also examine broader issues such as public relations, new market opportunities etc.

1
Sampling specific aspects of a company's environmental management in order to test efficiency and effectiveness of environmental protection and management.

Specific audits such as waste management, emissions controls, product liability etc.

Audits to identify major hazards associated with operations and means of reducing risk, eg loss control, land and groundwater contamination, pollution of rivers.

2
* Company policy, procedures and systems.
* Legal requirements
  * Limits on emissions etc.
* Authorisation and consent conditions.
* Public and customer attitudes.
* Other requirements: insurance, Shareholders

3
* Interviews: management, employees, representatives, enforcing agencies, community representatives.
* Sampling.
* Physical measurements.
* Observations.
* Records.
* Prosecutions, notices etc.

4
* Audit systems: Environment-CHASE, Environment-CATCH.
* In-house scoring systems, check-lists, etc.
* Outputs aim to disclose strengths and weaknesses and main areas of vulnerability and risk. Ranking of issues requiring detailed investigation/attention and recommended action lists.

5
* Policy changes.
* Enforcement of policy.
* Changes in procedures.
* Changes in responsibilities.
* Changes in systems of management. Remedial clean-up.
* Training.
* Communications.
* Insurance.
* Detailed assessments of risks identified. Etc.

6
* Audit teams including: Managers Environmental Advisers Specialists.

TYPE OF ASSESSMENT: Hazard Assessment - identification, assessment and control of major hazards to health, property and the environment. Can be applied to existing or planned development and may examine both internal and external conditions.

1
Routine workplace inspections to identify hazards and promote remedial action may include safety sampling, safety audits, safety inspections, hazard surveys, incident control etc.

Discussion between workers and management

Independent audits by engineering surveyors, employer's liability surveyors, claims investigators, insurance brokers, consultants, enforcing authorities.

2
* Forecast impact on company if no action taken.
* Codes of Practice.
* Legal requirements.

Reduction in accident costs/frequency.

Loss minimisation.

3
* Management structures.
* Safety management systems.
* Data on plant, equipment, guarding.
* Methods of operation.
* Observations eg forklift driving.
* Training programmes.
* Emergency plans/procedures.
* Process design.
* Layout/ construction of plant.
* Records eg accidents.
* Inspections - housekeeping.
* Workforce participation.

4
* Task safety analysis
* Hazard and Operability Study (HAZOP)
* Risk Assessment
* Assessment of probability that hazards will result in loss.
* Forecasting/ prediction eg dense gas cloud dispersal.

5
List of priorities for hazard controls and main control options including:
- elimination,
- reduction,
- remove employee,
- enclose hazard,
- protective equipment,
- permit-to-work system.

Timescales for control:
- immediate
- same day
- week
- etc.

6
* Specially convened teams including:
- employee representatives,
- managers,
- health and safety advisers,
- engineers,
- chemical engineers,
- production managers,
- designers, etc

* Responsible managers, supervisors and advisers may undertake on the spot appraisal in circumstances of immediate danger.

TYPE OF ASSESSMENT: Hazardous substances assessment - a systematic assessment procedure which identifies substances that are hazardous to health and safety within the workplace, the nature of the hazard and the risk to health and safety for employees and other affected, and the ways in which risks can be controlled. Can be applied in existing workplaces or in the planning of new facilities.

1
Inventory of all substances used or produced including raw materials, supplies, intermediates, by-products, products, wastes, emissions, contaminants, etc. Identification of those substances which are potentially hazardous to health and safety by way of their chemical or physical properties. May include gases, vapours, liquids, solids, dusts, fumes, microorganisms, and radiations.

Evidence of existence of health problems in the workplace.

Worker complaints or concerns.

Visible dusts present on surfaces and in the atmosphere.

Hazardous substances encountered during maintenance, demolition or construction including asbestos, lead etc.

2
- Occupational exposure limits, TLV.
* Background levels.
* Other sources of exposure.
* Other routes of exposure.
* Long-term health effects.
* Serious irreversible effects.
* Physical risks, explosion, fire.
* Corrosive, irritants.
* Sensitizing agents.
* Infectious agents.

3
* Substances:
  - previous experience,
  - supplier data,
  - official guidance,
  - approved lists,
  - codes of practice
  - nature of hazard
  - route of entry
  - immediate or delayed effects
  - chronic health effects.
  - carcinogens,
  mutagens,
  teratogens.
  - sensitization.
  - infectiousness.

4
* Potential of harm,
  - chance of exposure occurring, quantity and duration of exposure, need for control measures, need for health surveillance, need for workplace monitoring.
* Examine work patterns to identify:
  - who is exposed,
  - how long,
  - route of exposure,
  - working practices,
  - consequences of emergencies,
  - vulnerable individuals.

5
* Substitution.
* Elimination.
* Control measures
* Health surveillance.
* Exposure monitoring.
* Process change.
* Improved designs.
* Personal protective equipment.
* Training, information.
* Systems of work.
* Reduced time exposures.
* Employee selection.
* Insurance.

6
* Operators.
* Employee representatives.
* Managers.
* Designers.
* Architects.
* Occupational health specialists.
* Engineers.
* Enforcing authorities.

TYPE OF ASSESSMENT: Machinery hazards assessment – hazards and risks associated with machinery in the workplace environment with the objective of identifying conditions that may be prejudicial to health, safety or comfort.

1
Prosecutions or notices.

Observations/inspections indicating presence of revolving parts, abrasive wheels, reciprocating mechanisms, close nipping hazards, severance hazards, crushing hazards, non-mechanical hazards etc.

Accidents records.

Insurance claims.

2
* Are there:
  - traps,
  - impact hazards,
  - contact hazards,
  - entanglement hazards,
  - ejection hazards,
  - exposure hazards,
* Codes of practice.

3 * Routine inspection during normal and emergency operation.
* Observations eg operator behaviour.
* Interviews, questionnaires.
* Testing:
  - machines,
  - guards,
  - operators,
  - trips etc.
* Standards, etc.
* Comparative examples.

4 * Risk assessment of:
  - potential of harm,
  - form of hazard,
  - probability of failure
  - frequency of access,
  - proximity of access,
  - circumstances of access,
  - type of injuries.
* Assessment of build up of danger.
* Ease or use of machines and guards.
* Potential for operators to override safety features.
* Reliability of safeguards.

5 * Information/ education on risks to safety.
* Intrinsic safety.
* Minimise need for access.
* Guarding interlocked.
* Fencing.
* Trip devices.
* Location.
* Access restriction.
* Systems of work.
* Permit to work.
* Motivational training.
* Warning notices.
* Specification in purchasing.
* Fail safe systems.
* Planned maintenance.
* Ergonomic layout.
* Inspections, monitoring, audits etc.

6 * Operators.
* Employee representatives.
* Supervisors.
* Managers.
* Maintenance engineers.
* Engineers.
* Designers.
* Architects.
* Safety advisers.

TYPE OF ASSESSMENT: Ergonomic Assessment - assessment of the performance and needs of human beings within working environments including the study of relationships between people, the equipment with which they work and the physical environment within which they both operate.

1
- Increased injuries both as acute injuries such as cuts, bruises and fractures and chronic injuries including tenosynovitis, epicondylitis, back pain.
- Psychological problems such as stress, anxiety, etc.
- Poor performance from reduced output, increased errors, reduced quality, delayed response times.
- High turnover in staff and difficulties in recruitment.

2
* Functioning of devices under user control.
* Ease of use.
* Ease of learning.
* Attitudes.
* Straining/lifting hazards.
* Repetitive operations.
* "User friendly".
* Efficiency, effectiveness and economy.
* Attendance.
* Illness Rates.
* Insurance Claims.

3
* Data on tasks, responsibilities, job contexts etc.
* Measurements of spaces, sizes, timings, bodily dimensions, variation in people etc.
* Designer participation
* Simulation exercises.
* Observations of behaviour, movements.
* Interviews.
* Check-lists, diaries, questionnaires.
* Controlled experiments.
* Analysis of errors.
* Attitude surveys.

4
* Incidence of injuries.
* Task/job analysis.
* Layout analysis
* Physical ergonomic assessment incl:
  - design of workplaces,
  - work patterns,
  - work methods.
* Transactional analysis.
* Cognitive ergonomic assessment
* Human reliability analysis.
* Time line analysis.
* Psychological analysis.

5
* Employee selection for tasks.
* Task design.
* Systems of work.
* Design of workplace, tools, equipment, machines.
* Lifting aids.
* Instruction/training.
* Display information/readouts
* Motivation.
* Purchasing criteria.
* Design guidance.

6
* Operators.
* Employee representatives.
* Managers.
* Occupational Psychologists.
* Behavioural psychologists.
* Designers.
* Architects
* Occupational health specialists

TYPE OF ASSESSMENT: Air Quality Assessment - identification and assessment of the hazards and risks associated with atmospheric contaminants in the workplace environment and in the local environment with the objective of identifying conditions that may be prejudicial to health, safety or comfort or may have adverse effects on ecological systems, amenity or property.

1. Complaints about poor air quality, fumes, smells, dust, etc.

   Prosecutions or notices.

   Observations/inspections indicating presence of detectable fumes, mists, gases, dusts or fibres in the workplace atmosphere or conditions that may give rise to contamination of the atmosphere eg presence of asbestos products, volatile solvents, high temperature processes, foaming processes, stacks, vents, pressure relief systems, stock piles, vented storage areas, dusty surfaces etc.

   Accidents records, particularly gassing accidents or accidents influenced by exposure to contaminants.

   Insurance claims for occupational diseases or environmental damage.

   Epidemiological evidence of exposure.

   Absences/sickness records.

   Inventory of substances used as raw materials, process materials, supplies, products, wastes etc.

   Dust lamp surveys, simple indicator tubes surveys or dispersion tests using smoke tubes.

   Visible accumulations or deposition of fine dusts on surfaces etc.

   Presence of poorly ventilated or confined working areas.

   Risk assessment studies.

   Local environmental studies.

Continued on next page...

2	3	4	5	6
* Occupational exposure limits, TLV's etc. * Biological exposure limits, blood lead etc. * Minimum exposure to carcinogens, sensitizers etc. * Toxicological criteria, LD$_{50}$. * No effect levels. * Odour detection levels. * Acceptable daily intakes. * Presence/absence of infectious agents. * Presence of asphyxiation, explosion, flammable conditions. * Environmental quality standards. * Background levels. * Air quality objectives. * Qualitative criteria such as soiling rates.	* Measurements of emissions or ambient levels. * Personal exposure monitoring. * Air flow measurements. * Mass balances, emission rates, dilution estimates etc. * Behaviour studies. * Observations. * Occupational or environmental health records. * Medical/ biological monitoring and surveillance. * Complaints. * Sickness/absence records. * Design/ layout information. * Epidemiological studies. * Toxicity and ecotoxicity data. * Habitat surveys, species information etc. * Prediction/ modelling.	* Environmental impact assessment * Comparative risk analysis. * Assessment of: - potential of harm, - form of hazard, - probability of exposure - frequency of exposure, - possible mixed exposures, - circumstances of exposure, - type of injuries, effects, - exposures via other routes. - Cost benefit analysis. * Effectiveness of personal protective equipment. * Effectiveness of controls including: - dilution ventilation, - local exhaust ventilation, - containment, - isolation etc. * Cost benefit analysis.	* Information and education about potential risks to safety. * Inspections, monitoring, audits etc. * Pollution control devices. * Elimination, substitution or process change. * Control systems including dilution ventilation, local exhaust extraction, containment, isolation etc. * Reduced time exposure. * Medical surveillance. * Biological monitoring. * Training. * Monitoring of exposures. * Controlled access. * Personal protective equipment. * Entry checks for confined spaces etc. * Emergency plans. * Amelioration measures. * Habitat reinstatement. * Insurance. * Compensation	* Employees. * Employee representatives. * Supervisors. * Managers. * Enforcing authorities. * Designers. * Architects. Medical practitioners * Safety advisers. * Occupational hygienists. * Engineers * Insurers. * Planning authorities. * Environmental scientists. * Local community representatives.

TYPE OF ASSESSMENT: Noise Assessment - assessment of the levels of noise in the workplace environment and in the local community with the objective of identifying conditions that may be prejudicial to health, safety or comfort.

1
- Complaints from workers or local residents about high levels of noise, noise nuisance, or noise related health effects.
- Prosecutions or notices.
- Health records indicating excessive or increased frequency of noise induced health effects, such as occupational hearing loss, temporary threshold shift, tinnitus.
- Insurance claims.
- Poor performance, errors, poor quality etc.
- Accidents partly or wholly attributable to noise such as failure to hear alarms, warning shouts, falling machine etc.
- Initial surveys or monitoring.

2
* Noise rating curves.
* Sound pressure levels, dB's etc.
* Frequency, octave bands.
* First action level 85 dB(A) L_{eq}.
* Lowest achievable exposure.
* Noise emission limits for tools etc.
* Background levels.
* Planning conditions.
* Noise abatement zones.

3
* Measurements using noise meters, personal noise dose meters, frequency analysers.
* Audiograms.
* Manufacturers data, labels etc.
* Noise emission measurements and noise attenuation predictions.
* Noise modelling.
* Comparative data from similar situations.
* Observations.
* Interviews, questionnaires.

4
* Identification of all employees at risk.
* Noise rating curves.
* Impact assessment.

5
* Information and education about potential risks to health.
* Hearing protection.
* Ear protection zones.
* Safety signs.
* Standards for all purchasing.
* Control of noise at source.
* Vibration isolation.
* Vibration damping.
* Sound insulation.
* Sound absorption.
* Silencers/diffusers.
* Workplace layout/design.
* Regular checks/monitoring.

6
* Operators.
* Employee representatives.
* Managers.
* Maintenance engineers.
* Acousticians.
* Designers.
* Architects
* Occupational health specialists

TYPE OF ASSESSMENT: Lighting Assessment - assessment of the levels of illumination, contrast and colours in the working environment with the objective of identifying conditions that may be prejudicial to health, safety or comfort.

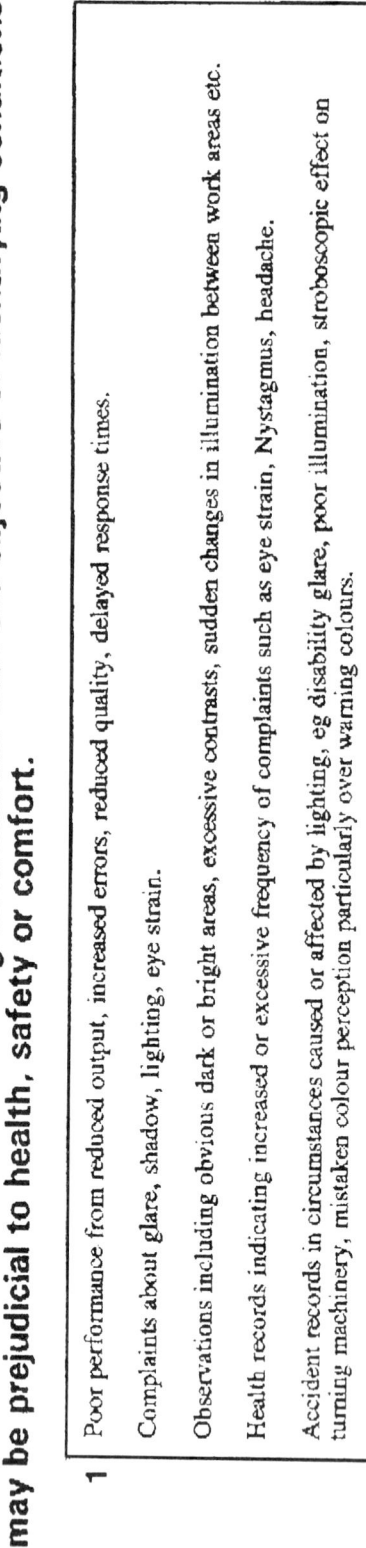

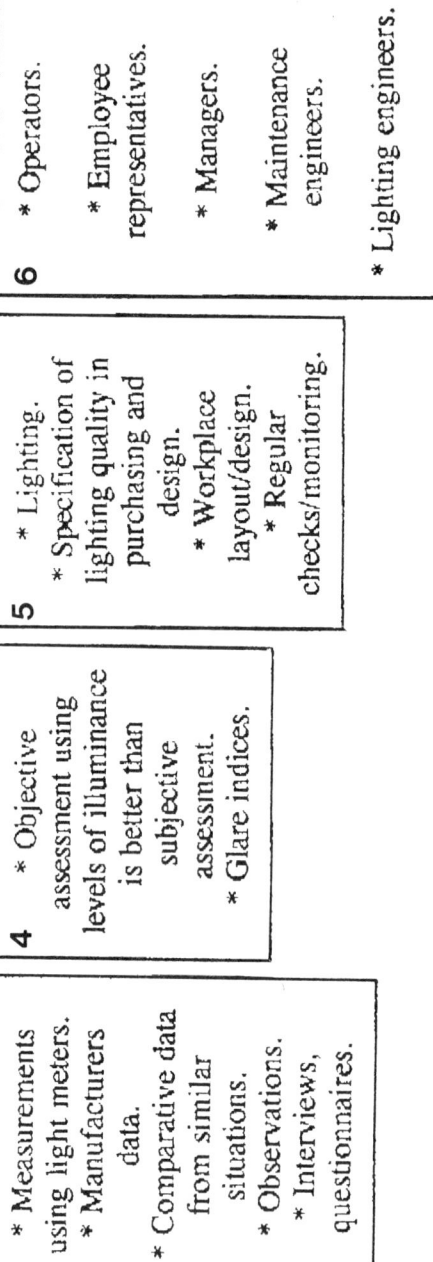

1
- Poor performance from reduced output, increased errors, reduced quality, delayed response times.
- Complaints about glare, shadow, lighting, eye strain.
- Observations including obvious dark or bright areas, excessive contrasts, sudden changes in illumination between work areas etc.
- Health records indicating increased or excessive frequency of complaints such as eye strain, Nystagmus, headache.
- Accident records in circumstances caused or affected by lighting, eg disability glare, poor illumination, stroboscopic effect on turning machinery, mistaken colour perception particularly over warning colours.

2
- * Standard service illuminance levels.
- * Contrast.
- * Reflection.
- * Glare.
- * Stroboscopic effect.
- * Colour contrast.

3
- * Measurements using light meters.
- * Manufacturers data.
- * Comparative data from similar situations.
- * Observations.
- * Interviews, questionnaires.

4
- * Objective assessment using levels of illuminance is better than subjective assessment.
- * Glare indices.

5
- * Lighting.
- * Specification of lighting quality in purchasing and design.
- * Workplace layout/design.
- * Regular checks/monitoring.

6
- * Operators.
- * Employee representatives.
- * Managers.
- * Maintenance engineers.
- * Lighting engineers.
- * Designers.
- * Architects
- * Occupational health specialists

TYPE OF ASSESSMENT: Environmental Impact Assessment - ex-ante assessment procedure designed to review proposed developments and identify potential environmental effects and the impact of those effects on natural resources, systems and process, the health and amenity of local populations, historical and cultural features etc.

1 Initial scoping stage to review project proposals and identify likely impacts for further detailed assessment. Consultation with concerned bodies, local communities and experts to identify main areas of concern.

Preliminary stages of assessment may also involve the identification of alternative options with respect to siting, processes, impact reduction controls, management, amelioration measures etc.

2
* Environmental quality standards for air, water, noise or land pollution.
* Planning constraints on traffic, noise, visual impact etc.
* Qualitative criteria such as impact on transboundary pollution, Global warming etc.
* Damage or disturbance to protected habitats or species, archaeology etc

3
* Data from similar operations elsewhere.
* Policies.
* Planning requirements.
* Predictions of emissions, wastes etc.
* Design specifications.
* Preiction/modelling of environmental impacts.
* Measurement/surveys of baseline environmental conditions.
* Observations.
* Interviews.

4 Environmental statement summarising the impacts on:
- air quality,
- climate,
- noise/vibration,
- water,
- land,
- ecology,
- human populations,
- geology,
- heritage,
- landscape,
- recreation etc.

Matrix summaries of impacts for each design option can be used to analyse interactions, higher order impacts etc.

5
* Impact matrix used to give most favourable project design.
* For areas of significant impact, control options can be identified including:
- alternative site,
- emission controls,
- landscaping,
- habitat protection,
- routing traffic flows,
- restrict operating times,
- alternative raw materials,
- waste minimisation etc

6
* Environmental impact assessment team including:
- environmental scientists
- engineers
- planners
- ecologists
- social scientists
- lawyers
- architects
- chemical engineers
- designers etc.

*Environmental statement independently appraised by local planning authority, statutory bodies etc.

TYPE OF ASSESSMENT: Health Assessment - assessment designed to identify and investigate causal relationships between exposure to health hazards arising from work activities and adverse effects on health and well being. Assessment may be directed at workers, former workers or neighbouring communities.

1
- Increased or excessive accident rates.
- Increase or excessive frequency of illness or death rates among the local population or workforce.
- Epidemiological evidence.
- Complaints and concerns about ill-health, the work environment or the local environment.
- Prosecutions or notices relating to health of workers or local residents.
- Findings of toxicological studies of substances used or emitted to the environment.

2
- * Accident rates.
- * Death rates (SMR's).
- * Insurance claims.
- * Comparative risk estimates.
- * Disease counts and health indicators.

3
- * Biological monitoring (eg blood lead).
- * Health records.
- * Exposure records.
- * Medical surveillance records.
- * Sickness/absence records.
- * Registers of disease/death.
- * Controlled experiments.
- * Epidemiological studies.
- * Questionnaires.
- * Interviews.
- * Process records.

4
- * Incidence of diseases.
- * Comparative health assessments.
- * Risk analysis.
- * Proportionate mortality analysis.
- * Multivariate analysis.
- * SMR etc.
- * Cost-benefit analysis.

5
- * Elimination
- * Substitution
- * Exposure controls.
- * Employee selection/exclsuion.
- * Personal protective equipment.
- * Engineering controls.
- * Setting/amending control limits
- * Process control/design.
- * Operation design.
- * Health screening.
- * Training/information
- * Insurance.
- * Compensation.
- * Decontamination.

6
- * Employees and representatives.
- * Medical practitioners.
- * Occupational hygienists.
- * Epidemiologists.
- * Enforcing authorities.
- * Insurers.
- * Health and Safety Advisers.
- * Local environmental health specialists/officers.

Appendix IV

Experience from practice.

EX:1459

TN1459
HS013

PRODUCT: CHROME ALI CLEAN

---

1. GENERAL DESCRIPTION

An aqueous acid (Orthophosphoric) detergent mixture.

---

2. HEALTH DATA

This product is classified as being Corrosive. Contact with eyes will cause severe irritation and may lead to permanent damage if First Aid treatment is not administered immediately. Skin contact with this product will cause irritation and may, if not treated, cause burns. Effects from the inhalation of mist varies from mild irritation of the nose to pneumonitis. Therefore to provide staff with prudent safety advice, personal protective equipment must be worn, see below for details.

EXPOSURE LIMITS: ORTHOPHOSPHORIC ACID, OES, $1 mgm^{-3}$ (8 hour), $3 mgm^{-3}$ (10 min).

---

3. PROTECTION DATA

3.1 Local Exhaust Ventilation: Ensure good ventilation.

3.2 Personal Protective Equipment, see safety equipment manual for details of codes.

3.2.1 HANDS: PPE122   3.2.2 EYES: PPE211 or 220 type or safety spectacles

3.2.3 RESPIRATORY: PPE333 if required   3.2.4 OTHER: -

---

4. EMERGENCY PROCEDURE DATA

4.1 First Aid:
   Eyes: Seek the attention of a First Aider IMMEDIATELY. Irrigate with plenty of clean water for at least 15 minutes.
   Skin: Seek the attention of a First Aider IMMEDIATELY. Remove contaminated clothing, wash the affected area with water for at least 15 minutes.

4.2 Spillage:
   LESS THAN 5Lts: wash to drain with plenty of water, taking care to avoid foam nuisance.
   MORE THAN 5Lts: Prevent product from entering drains. Seek IMMEDIATE advice from your supervisor.

---

5. CLEAN UP/DISPOSAL

Drain well, rinse with water and collect as aqueous waste. Flush with plenty of water to drain, taking care to avoid foam nuisance.

---

6. HAZARD CLASS

CORROSIVE

SEE MSDS: 1459 (for full details)	ISSUE No: 1
SIGNED:	DATE: July 1991

Fig. 1. *Example of a tank safety notice showing information on health and safety*
(Copyright: The Kent Chemical Company Ltd.)

PRODUCT MATERIAL SAFETY DATA SHEET	MSDS1459
	HS010

EX:1459

PRODUCT: CHROME ALI CLEAN

1. GENERAL DESCRIPTION
An aqueous acid (Orthophosporic) detergent mixture.

2. PHYSICAL DATA

2.1 **Form:** Liquid 2.2 **Colour:** Blue

2.3 **Odour:** Mildly acidic

2.4 **Density:** 1.18 Kg/Litre @ 20°C 2.5 **pH:** < 1, neat @ 20°C

3. HEALTH HAZARDS
This product is classified as being Corrosive. Contact with eyes will cause severe irritation and may lead to permanent damage if First Aid treatment is not administered immediately. Skin contact with this product will cause irritation and may, if not treated, cause burns. Inhalation of the vapour may cause burns to the respiratory tract, resulting in shortness of breath. Therefore to provide staff with prudent safety advice, personal protective equipment must be worn, see below for details.
EXPOSURE LIMITS: ORTHOPHOSPHORIC ACID, OES, 1mgm^{-3} (8 hour), 3mgm^{-3} (10 min).

4. PROTECTIVE MEASURES

4.1 **Storage:**
Store in closed, original container in a cool place under cover and away from strongly oxidising substances. Do not store with alkaline or formaldehyde containing materials. Protect from freezing.

4.2 **Handling:**
Ensure good ventilation to maintain the atmosphere below the Occupational Exposure Standard (OES). If this is not possible, a suitable respirator should be worn. Avoid skin contact wear suitable gloves. Take care to avoid spashing or contact with eyes. Wear suitable eye protection. Do not handle near alkalis.

4.3 **Local Exhaust Ventilation:**
Ensure good ventilation to maintain atmospheric concentrations below the Occupational Exposure Standards (OES)

4.3 **Personal Protective Equipment:**

Hands: Type PPE110 or 120   Eyes: PPE211 or 220 type
                                       or safety spectacles
Respiratory: PPE333   Other: Chemical apron

Fig. 2 Product safety data sheet - page 1
(Copyright: The Kent Chemical Company Ltd.)

To be continued....

| | MSDS1459 |
| PRODUCT MATERIAL SAFETY DATA SHEET | HS010 |

5. EMERGENCY PROCEDURE

5.1 Flash Point, °C: Non-Flammable

5.2 Fire Fighting Procedure:
Although this product is not in its self flammable the following extinguishing media may be used on fires involving this product:

    Water fog: Yes CO_2: Yes

    Foam: Yes   Dry powder: Yes

5.3 First Aid:
Eyes: Seek the attention of a First Aider **IMMEDIATELY**. Irrigate with plenty of clean water for least 15 minutes.
Skin: Seek the attention of a First Aider. Remove contaminated clothing, wash the affected area with water for at least 15 minutes.
Ingestion: Seek the attention of a First Aider **IMMEDIATELY**. DO NOT INDUCE VOMITING Rinse the mouth out several times with water and spit out. Give a pint of water to drink.
Inhalation: Remove victim from contaminated area. Seek the attention of a First Aider **IMMEDIATELY**.

5.4 Spills/Leaks:
LESS THAN 5Lts: wash to drain with plenty of water, taking care to avoid foam nuisance.
MORE THAN 5Lts: Wear appropriate safety protective equipment. Contain spillage with sand, to prevent product from entering drains. Neutralise very carefully by speading soda ash liberally over the spillage (test with litmus paper - red to blue). Add a large volume of water to the neutralised solution and wash to drain with plenty of water. Scrub area with water to remove residue.

6. CLEAN UP/DISPOSAL PROCEDURE

6.1 Clean up of equipment and disposal of material:

Drain well, rinse with water and collect as acid waste. Flush with plenty of water to drain, taking care to avoid foam nuisance.

6.2 Disposal of container:

Drain container well. Collect as acid waste. Flush container with plenty of water to drain. Dispose of container in chemical skip.

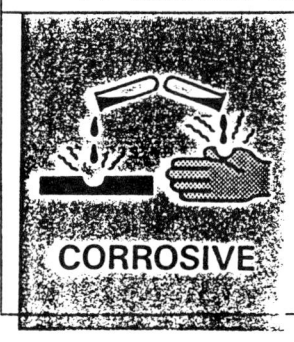

7. HAZARD CLASS

CORROSIVE

WHEN MANUFACTURING
USE TANK NOTICE: TN1459

WHEN FILLING
USE LINE NOTICE: LN1459

ISSUE No:	1
SIGNED:	
DATE:	March 1991

***Fig. 2** Product safety data sheet - page 2.*
(Copyright: The Kent Chemical Company Ltd.)

European Foundation for the Improvement of Living and Working Conditions

Workplace Assessment

Luxembourg: Office for Official Publications of the European Communities

1992 — 120 p. — 29.7 × 21 cm

ISBN 92-826-4858-3

Price (excluding VAT) in Luxembourg: ECU 12

Venta y suscripciones · Salg og abonnement · Verkauf und Abonnement · Πωλήσεις και συνδρομές · Sales and subscriptions · Vente et abonnements · Vendita e abbonamenti · Verkoop en abonnementen · Venda e assinaturas

BELGIQUE / BELGIË

**Moniteur belge /
Belgisch Staatsblad**
Rue de Louvain 42 / Leuvenseweg 42
1000 Bruxelles / 1000 Brussel
Tél. (02) 512 00 26
Fax 511 01 84
CCP / Postrekening 000-2005502-27

Autres distributeurs /
Overige verkooppunten

**Librairie européenne/
Europese Boekhandel**
Avenue Albert Jonnart 50 /
Albert Jonnartlaan 50
1200 Bruxelles / 1200 Brussel
Tél. (02) 734 02 81
Fax 735 08 60

Jean De Lannoy
Avenue du Roi 202 /Koningslaan 202
1060 Bruxelles / 1060 Brussel
Tél. (02) 538 51 69
Télex 63220 UNBOOK B
Fax (02) 538 08 41

CREDOC
Rue de la Montagne 34 / Bergstraat 34
Bte 11 / Bus 11
1000 Bruxelles / 1000 Brussel

DANMARK

**J. H. Schultz Information A/S
EF-Publikationer**
Ottiliavej 18
2500 Valby
Tlf. 36 44 22 66
Fax 36 44 01 41
Girokonto 6 00 08 86

BR DEUTSCHLAND

Bundesanzeiger Verlag
Breite Straße
Postfach 10 80 06
5000 Köln 1
Tel. (02 21) 20 29-0
Telex ANZEIGER BONN 8 882 595
Fax 20 29 278

GREECE/ΕΛΛΑΔΑ

G.C. Eleftheroudakis SA
International Bookstore
Nikis Street 4
10563 Athens
Tel. (01) 322 63 23
Telex 219410 ELEF
Fax 323 98 21

ESPAÑA

Boletín Oficial del Estado
Trafalgar, 27
28010 Madrid
Tel. (91) 44 82 135

Mundi-Prensa Libros, S.A.
Castelló, 37
28001 Madrid
Tel. (91) 431 33 99 (Libros)
431 32 22 (Suscripciones)
435 36 37 (Dirección)
Télex 49370-MPLI-E
Fax (91) 575 39 98

Sucursal:

Librería Internacional AEDOS
Consejo de Ciento, 391
08009 Barcelona
Tel. (93) 301 86 15
Fax (93) 317 01 41

**Llibreria de la Generalitat
de Catalunya**
Rambla dels Estudis, 118 (Palau Moja)
08002 Barcelona
Tel. (93) 302 68 35
302 64 62
Fax (93) 302 12 99

FRANCE

**Journal officiel
Service des publications
des Communautés européennes**
26, rue Desaix
75727 Paris Cedex 15
Tél. (1) 40 58 75 00
Fax (1) 40 58 75 74

IRELAND

Government Supplies Agency
4-5 Harcourt Road
Dublin 2
Tel. (1) 61 31 11
Fax (1) 78 06 45

ITALIA

Licosa Spa
Via Duca di Calabria, 1/1
Casella postale 552
50125 Firenze
Tel. (055) 64 54 15
Fax 64 12 57
Telex 570466 LICOSA I
CCP 343 509

GRAND-DUCHÉ DE LUXEMBOURG

Messageries Paul Kraus
11, rue Christophe Plantin
2339 Luxembourg
Tél. 499 88 88
Télex 2515
Fax 499 88 84 44
CCP 49242-63

NEDERLAND

SDU Overheidsinformatie
Externe Fondsen
Postbus 20014
2500 EA 's-Gravenhage
Tel. (070) 37 89 911
Fax (070) 34 75 778

PORTUGAL

Imprensa Nacional
Casa da Moeda, EP
Rua D. Francisco Manuel de Melo, 5
1092 Lisboa Codex
Tel. (01) 69 34 14

**Distribuidora de Livros
Bertrand, Ld.ª**
Grupo Bertrand, SA
Rua das Terras dos Vales, 4-A
Apartado 37
2700 Amadora Codex
Tel. (01) 49 59 050
Telex 15798 BERDIS
Fax 49 60 255

UNITED KINGDOM

HMSO Books (PC 16)
HMSO Publications Centre
51 Nine Elms Lane
London SW8 5DR
Tel. (071) 873 2000
Fax GP3 873 8463
Telex 29 71 138

ÖSTERREICH

**Manz'sche Verlags-
und Universitätsbuchhandlung**
Kohlmarkt 16
1014 Wien
Tel. (0222) 531 61-0
Telex 11 25 00 BOX A
Fax (0222) 531 61-39

SUOMI

Akateeminen Kirjakauppa
Keskuskatu 1
PO Box 128
00101 Helsinki
Tel. (0) 121 41
Fax (0) 121 44 41

NORGE

Narvesen information center
Bertrand Narvesens vei 2
PO Box 6125 Etterstad
0602 Oslo 6
Tel. (2) 57 33 00
Telex 79668 NIC N
Fax (2) 68 19 01

SVERIGE

BTJ
Box 200
22100 Lund
Tel. (046) 18 00 00
Fax (046) 18 01 25

SCHWEIZ / SUISSE / SVIZZERA

OSEC
Stampfenbachstraße 85
8035 Zürich
Tel. (01) 365 54 49
Fax (01) 365 54 11

CESKOSLOVENSKO

NIS
Havelkova 22
13000 Praha 3
Tel. (02) 235 84 46
Fax 42-2-264775

MAGYARORSZÁG

Euro-Info-Service
Budapest I. Kir.
Attila út 93
1012 Budapest
Tel. (1) 56 82 11
Telex (22) 4717 AGINF H-61
Fax (1) 17 59 031

POLSKA

Business Foundation
ul. Krucza 38/42
00-512 Warszawa
Tel. (22) 21 99 93, 628-28-82
International Fax&Phone
(0-39) 12-00-77

JUGOSLAVIJA

Privredni Vjesnik
Bulevar Lenjina 171/XIV
11070 Beograd
Tel. (11) 123 23 40

CYPRUS

Cyprus Chamber of Commerce and Industry
Chamber Building
38 Grivas Dhigenis Ave
3 Deligiorgis Street
PO Box 1455
Nicosia
Tel. (2) 449500/462312
Fax (2) 458630

TÜRKIYE

**Pres Gazete Kitap Dergi
Pazarlama Dağitim Ticaret ve sanayi
AŞ**
Narlibahçe Sokak N. 15
Istanbul-Cağaloğlu
Tel. (1) 520 92 96 - 528 55 66
Fax 520 64 57
Telex 23822 DSVO-TR

CANADA

Renouf Publishing Co. Ltd
Mail orders — Head Office:
1294 Algoma Road
Ottawa, Ontario K1B 3W8
Tel. (613) 741 43 33
Fax (613) 741 54 39
Telex 0534783

Ottawa Store:
61 Sparks Street
Tel. (613) 238 89 85

Toronto Store:
211 Yonge Street
Tel. (416) 363 31 71

UNITED STATES OF AMERICA

UNIPUB
4611-F Assembly Drive
Lanham, MD 20706-4391
Tel. Toll Free (800) 274 4888
Fax (301) 459 0056

AUSTRALIA

Hunter Publications
58A Gipps Street
Collingwood
Victoria 3066

JAPAN

Kinokuniya Company Ltd
17-7 Shinjuku 3-Chome
Shinjuku-ku
Tokyo 160-91
Tel. (03) 3439-0121

Journal Department
PO Box 55 Chitose
Tokyo 156
Tel. (03) 3439-0124

AUTRES PAYS
OTHER COUNTRIES
ANDERE LÄNDER

**Office des publications officielles
des Communautés européennes**
2, rue Mercier
2985 Luxembourg
Tél. 49 92 81
Télex PUBOF LU 1324 b
Fax 48 85 73/48 68 17
CC bancaire BIL 8-109/6003/700

12/91